INTERESTING
FACTS FOR THE CURIOUS – USA

VOLUME 3

FROM ILLINOIS TO MISSOURI
JP MORIARTY

© 2024 by JP Moriarty

No part of this book may be used or reproduced in any manner whatsoever without written permission except in the case of brief quotations embodied in critical articles and reviews.

INTERESTING
FACTS FOR THE CURIOUS – USA

VOLUME 3

Contents

INTRODUCTION vii

01: MONTANA 1

02: NEBRASKA 24

03: NEVADA 45

04: NEW HAMPSHIRE 65

05: NEW JERSEY 86

06: NEW MEXICO 104

07: NEW YORK 127

08: NORTH CAROLINA 149

09: NORTH DAKOTA 171

10: OHIO 195

11: OKLAHOMA 217

12: OREGON 240

13: PENNSYLVANIA 263

Introduction

Welcome explorers, to Volume 3 of "Interesting Facts for the Curious - USA" This journey through the wonders of America is crafted especially for those of you with a keen eye for the peculiar and a mind eager to unravel the mysteries of the world around us. Whatever age you are, there's something in these pages that will ignite your curiosity and feed your hunger for knowledge.

Have you ever wondered why some facts stick with us, making us say "Wow!" while others just slip away? The secret lies in their ability to spark our imagination and lead us down pathways of discovery. Facts that surprise us, that reveal something hidden or unexpected, are like treasures waiting to be found. They make us think, ask questions, and seek out more knowledge.

Curiosity is the driving force behind all learning. As Zora Neale Hurston wisely said, "Research is formalized curiosity. It is poking and prying with a purpose." This book series is your guide to poking and prying into the fascinating details of each state in the USA. You'll find intriguing stories, unusual records, and quirky bits of history that showcase the unique character of each place.

"From the smallest necessity to the highest religious abstraction, from the wheel to the skyscraper, everything we are and everything we have comes from one attribute of man – the function of his reasoning mind," said Ayn Rand. This powerful idea reminds us that our ability to reason and question is at the heart of all progress and discovery. It's our curiosity that drives us to explore, invent, and understand the world.

In this volume, you'll embark on an adventure through states filled with surprising facts. You'll discover who was the first woman elected to congress, where the vise-grip was invented and in what state plywood was first shown to the public. You'll learn about states where nation-defining events took place, states with unique character and with natural wonders that will make you marvel at the diversity and creativity found across the USA.

As you turn each page, remember that every fact you read is a doorway to a new adventure. Let your curiosity guide you, ask questions, and seek out the stories behind the facts. This book isn't just about memorizing information; it's about inspiring you to think deeply, explore widely, and embrace the joy of discovery.

So, buckle up and get ready to explore the incredible and intriguing facts that make each state in the USA a unique part of this nation's tapestry. Let your curiosity lead the way and enjoy the journey!

Happy exploring,

Jonathan

01

MONTANA

1. Jeannette Rankin: Trailblazer for Women in Politics

Jeannette Rankin was a pioneering force in American politics, making history as the first woman elected to the United States Congress in 1916. Born in Missoula, Montana, in 1880, Rankin's journey to political prominence was fueled by her passion for social reform and women's rights. She graduated from the University of Montana in 1902 and later attended the New York School of Philanthropy, where she honed her advocacy skills.

Rankin's election to Congress was a monumental achievement, considering women did not yet have the right to vote nationwide. Her victory was a testament to her relentless campaigning and the support she garnered from women and progressive men. In

Congress, Rankin was a staunch advocate for peace and social justice. She was one of the few members who voted against U.S. entry into World War I and, later, World War II, reflecting her deep pacifist beliefs.

Rankin's legacy extends beyond her congressional service. She was a key figure in the women's suffrage movement, tirelessly working to secure voting rights for women. Her activism played a significant role in the passage of the 19th Amendment in 1920, which granted women the right to vote. Rankin's dedication to social causes continued throughout her life, including advocating for civil rights and opposing U.S. military interventions.

Jeannette Rankin's life and career exemplify courage and conviction. She broke barriers and laid the groundwork for future generations of women in politics. Her unwavering commitment to peace and equality remains an inspiring legacy, highlighting the profound impact one determined individual can have on society.

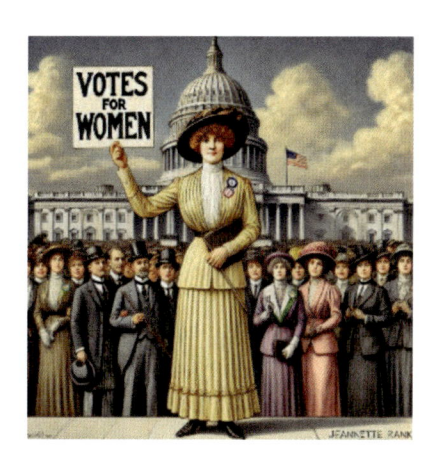

2. Automatic Gas Pump: The first automatic gas pump was invented by a Montana resident, Carl Kiekhaefer. This invention revolutionized the way gas stations operated by allowing self-service fueling.

3. Smokejumpers: The concept of smokejumpers, firefighters who parachute into remote areas to combat wildfires, was pioneered in Montana in the 1940s. This method has since become an essential part of wildfire management.

4. Rescue Fire Shelters: The development of lightweight, portable fire shelters, essential for firefighter safety, was significantly advanced in Montana due to the state's frequent and severe wildfires.

5. Evel Knievel: The Daredevil from Butte

Evel Knievel, born Robert Craig Knievel Jr. in 1938 in Butte, Montana, became a legendary figure known for his daring motorcycle stunts and flamboyant personality. His career as a stunt performer captured the imagination of millions and cemented his status as an American icon.

Knievel's journey to fame began in the 1960s when he started performing motorcycle jumps at small venues. His fearless nature and showmanship quickly gained attention, leading to increasingly ambitious stunts. Knievel's reputation soared with his televised jumps, including his attempt to jump the fountains at Caesars Palace in Las Vegas in 1967. Although the jump ended in a dramatic crash, it made Knievel a household name.

Throughout the 1970s, Knievel's stunts grew more daring, with jumps over cars, buses, and even a canyon. His most famous and controversial stunt was the Snake River Canyon jump in 1974, where he attempted to cross the canyon in a steam-powered rocket. Despite the jump's failure, Knievel's willingness to push the boundaries of what was possible resonated with fans around the world.

Knievel's impact extended beyond his stunts. He became a symbol of fearlessness and determination, inspiring countless people to pursue their dreams despite the risks. His colorful personality and media savvy also made him a pop culture phenomenon, leading to merchandise, movies, and television appearances.

Despite numerous injuries and crashes, Knievel's legacy endures as a testament to human courage and resilience. He passed away in 2007, but his influence on the world of extreme sports and entertainment continues to be felt. Evel Knievel's life story is a thrilling testament to the spirit of adventure and the pursuit of greatness.

6. The Clark Fork River: Flowing through western Montana, the Clark Fork River is known for its scenic beauty and recreational opportunities, including fishing, rafting, and kayaking.

7. Virginia City: A well-preserved ghost town, Virginia City offers a glimpse into Montana's gold rush era with historic buildings, museums, and reenactments.

8. Helena Gold Rush: The discovery of gold in Helena in 1864 led to a significant gold rush, establishing the city as

Montana's capital and a key economic center during the 19th century.

9. Montana Territory: The Montana Territory was established in 1864, carved out of the larger Idaho Territory, and included parts of modern-day Montana, Wyoming, and North Dakota.

10. The Garden of One Thousand Buddhas: A Place of Peace and Meditation

Nestled in the Jocko Valley of Arlee, Montana, the Garden of One Thousand Buddhas is a serene and spiritually enriching destination. This sacred site, developed by the Tibetan Lama Tshedrub Yeshe, aims to inspire peace, compassion, and wisdom. The garden's design is based on the eight-spoked Dharma wheel, a significant symbol in Buddhism, representing the Noble Eightfold Path to enlightenment.

The garden features 1,000 statues of Buddha, each meticulously crafted to represent different aspects of Buddhist teachings. Surrounding a central statue of Yum Chenmo, the Great Mother, the Buddhas are arranged in a circular formation, symbolizing the unity and interconnectedness of all beings. Visitors often find a sense of tranquility and introspection as they walk among the statues, with the beautiful Montana landscape providing a stunning backdrop.

The Garden of One Thousand Buddhas is not only a place for meditation and reflection but also a center for cultural and educational activities. It hosts teachings, workshops, and ceremonies that promote understanding and appreciation of Buddhist principles. The garden's inclusive philosophy welcomes people of all backgrounds and beliefs, encouraging a universal message of peace and compassion.

In addition to its spiritual significance, the garden plays a vital role in the local community. It attracts visitors from around the world, contributing to the cultural and economic vitality of the region. The garden's creation has also fostered a sense of collaboration and respect among the diverse communities in Montana.

Visiting the Garden of One Thousand Buddhas offers a unique opportunity to experience a profound sense of peace and connection. It stands as a testament to the power of compassion and the universal quest for enlightenment.

11. Glacier National Park: Known as the "Crown of the Continent," Glacier National Park boasts stunning landscapes, diverse wildlife, and over 700 miles of hiking trails. It's home to the famous Going-to-the-Sun Road.

12. Big Sky Country: Montana is often called "Big Sky Country" due to its vast, open landscapes and expansive skies. The state's stunning scenery includes prairies, mountains, and forests.

13. Flathead Lake: The largest natural freshwater lake in the western United States, Flathead Lake is known for its crystal-clear waters and recreational opportunities, including boating and fishing.

14. Statehood: Montana became the 41st state of the United States on November 8, 1889. Its admission marked a significant moment in the westward expansion of the country.

15. The Continental Divide: Nature's Great Divide

The Continental Divide is one of North America's most significant natural landmarks, and it plays a crucial role in Montana's geography and ecology. This major hydrological divide runs along the crest of the Rocky Mountains, separating the watersheds that drain into the Pacific Ocean from those that drain into the Atlantic Ocean and the Gulf of Mexico. In

Montana, the divide stretches from the Canadian border in the north, traversing through the heart of the Rocky Mountains, down to the border with Wyoming.

The Continental Divide in Montana is a place of stunning natural beauty and ecological diversity. It encompasses some of the state's most famous natural attractions, including Glacier National Park and the Bob Marshall Wilderness. These areas are home to a variety of wildlife, such as grizzly bears, mountain goats, and elk, and feature dramatic landscapes of rugged peaks, alpine meadows, and crystal-clear lakes.

One of the most iconic locations along the divide is Triple Divide Peak in Glacier National Park. From this unique summit, waters flow into three different oceans: the Pacific, the Atlantic, and the Arctic, making it one of the only places in the world with this distinction. Hiking the Continental Divide Trail, which runs through Montana, offers adventurers an unparalleled experience of the state's wilderness, with breathtaking views and challenging terrain.

The Continental Divide is not just a physical landmark but also a symbol of the diverse and interconnected ecosystems that make up the region. It represents the natural division and distribution of water resources, which are vital for the environment and the communities that depend on them.

Exploring the Continental Divide provides a deeper appreciation of Montana's natural heritage and the intricate balance of its ecosystems. It's a reminder of the powerful forces of nature that shape our world.

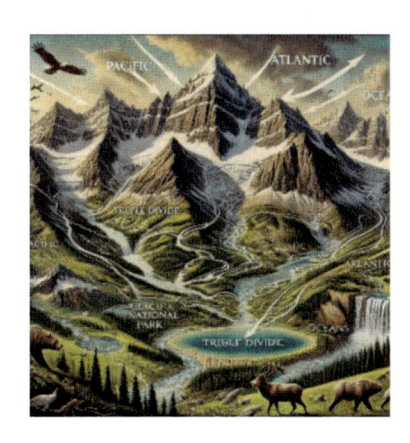

16. Gary Cooper: Born in Helena, Gary Cooper was a legendary Hollywood actor known for his roles in classic films such as "High Noon" and "Sergeant York." He won two Academy Awards for Best Actor.

17. Aerated Water (Carbonated): John Matthews, from Bozeman, Montana, developed one of the early versions of carbonated water, contributing to the popularity of soda beverages.

18. C.M. Russell: Charles Marion Russell, known as the "Cowboy Artist," lived in Great Falls, Montana. His paintings and sculptures of cowboys, Native Americans, and Western landscapes are world-famous.

19. The Holter Monitor: A Revolution in Cardiac Care

The Holter monitor, a groundbreaking medical device used for continuous monitoring of heart activity, was invented by Dr. Norman J. Holter, a physicist from Helena, Montana. Introduced in 1949, this portable device revolutionized cardiac care by allowing doctors to track the heart's electrical activity over an extended period, usually 24 to 48 hours. This was a significant advancement over the short-term electrocardiograms (ECGs) previously used, which only provided a brief snapshot of heart function.

Dr. Holter's innovation came from his interest in both science and medicine. He aimed to create a device that could non-invasively monitor heart activity, providing valuable data for diagnosing and managing heart conditions. The original Holter monitor was quite cumbersome, weighing around 75 pounds and requiring patients to carry the equipment in a backpack. Over time, technological advancements have made the device much smaller and more convenient, with modern versions being lightweight and wearable on the chest.

The Holter monitor works by using electrodes attached to the patient's chest to detect and record the heart's electrical impulses. The data is then analyzed by healthcare professionals to identify irregularities such as arrhythmias, silent heart attacks, and other cardiac issues. This continuous monitoring is crucial for diagnosing conditions that might not be apparent during a brief examination.

Dr. Holter's invention has saved countless lives and remains a vital tool in cardiology. His work exemplifies the spirit of innovation and dedication to improving human health. The Holter monitor not only enhanced our understanding of heart function but also paved the way for further developments in portable medical technology.

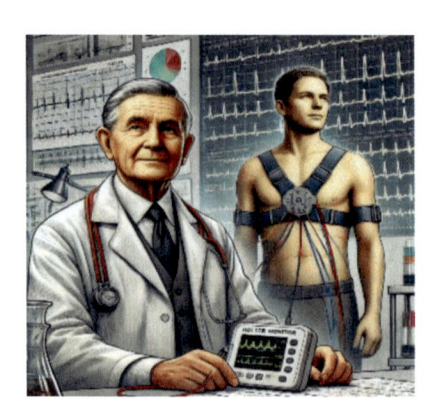

20. Montana's State Quarter: Designed in 2007, the Montana state quarter features a bison skull over a landscape, symbolizing the state's rich Native American heritage and natural beauty.

21. LLivingston's Literary Scene: Livingston, Montana, is known for its vibrant literary community. Famous writers like Richard Ford and Jim Harrison have lived and written there, contributing to its reputation as a creative hub.

22. Museum of the Rockies: Located in Bozeman, this museum is renowned for its extensive collection of dinosaur fossils and exhibits on Native American culture, the history of the West, and the state's natural history.

23. Missouri River: The Missouri River, which begins in Montana, is the longest river in North America. It played a significant role in the exploration and development of the western United States.

24. Phil Jackson: The Zen Master of Basketball

Phil Jackson, one of the most successful and respected coaches in NBA history, was born in Deer Lodge, Montana, in 1945. Known as the "Zen Master" for his unique coaching style that incorporates principles of mindfulness and meditation, Jackson's influence on basketball is profound. He led the Chicago Bulls and the Los Angeles Lakers to a combined 11 NBA championships, making him the coach with the most titles in NBA history.

Jackson's journey to becoming a legendary coach began as a player. He played college basketball at the University of North Dakota before joining the New York Knicks, where he won two NBA championships as a player. His coaching career took off when he became head coach of the Chicago Bulls in 1989. Under his leadership, the Bulls, led by Michael Jordan, won six NBA championships in the 1990s.

In 1999, Jackson took over as head coach of the Los Angeles Lakers, where he guided the team to five more championships. His coaching philosophy, which emphasizes teamwork, mental toughness, and holistic well-being, set him apart. Jackson's approach includes elements of Eastern philosophy, Native American traditions, and the use of meditation techniques to help players stay focused and cohesive.

Jackson's legacy extends beyond his championships. He is known for developing the "Triangle Offense," a strategic system that maximizes player movement and spacing. His ability to manage superstar players and foster a team-first mentality earned him respect and admiration across the sports world.

Phil Jackson's influence on basketball continues through his books and mentorship of younger coaches. His unique blend of strategy, psychology, and spirituality has left an indelible mark on the game, inspiring future generations of players and coaches.

25. Homestead Act: The Homestead Act of 1862 encouraged settlement in Montana by offering land to settlers willing to cultivate it. This led to a significant influx of homesteaders in the late 19th and early 20th centuries.

26. The Battle of Little Bighorn: Custer's Last Stand

The Battle of Little Bighorn, often referred to as "Custer's Last Stand," is one of the most famous and significant conflicts in American history. Fought on June 25-26, 1876, near the Little Bighorn River in southeastern Montana Territory, it was a pivotal moment in the Great Sioux War of 1876.

The battle was between the United States Army's 7th Cavalry, led by Lieutenant Colonel George Armstrong Custer, and a coalition of Native American tribes, including the Lakota Sioux, Northern Cheyenne, and Arapaho. The Native American forces were led by prominent leaders such as Sitting Bull, Crazy Horse, and Chief Gall. Tensions had escalated due to the U.S. government's encroachment on Native lands, particularly after gold was discovered in the Black Hills, an area sacred to the Lakota.

Custer, known for his aggressive tactics, underestimated the strength and resolve of the Native American warriors. He divided his forces, aiming for a quick and decisive victory. However, the Native American coalition, vastly outnumbering Custer's troops, launched a fierce and coordinated counterattack. The battle resulted in the complete annihilation of Custer's detachment, with over 200 soldiers killed, including Custer himself.

The victory at Little Bighorn was a momentous triumph for the Native American tribes, symbolizing their resistance and bravery. However, it also led to a relentless military campaign by the U.S. government to subdue the tribes and force them onto reservations. The battle marked the beginning of the end for the Plains Indians' way of life.

Today, the Little Bighorn Battlefield National Monument stands as a tribute to both the U.S. soldiers and the Native American warriors who fought there. It serves as a reminder of the complex and often tragic history of westward expansion and the enduring spirit of the Native American people.

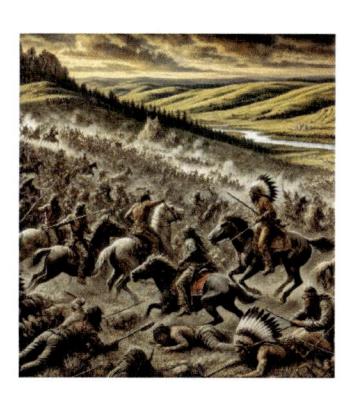

27. Streamlined Snowmobile: The development of the modern, streamlined snowmobile was significantly advanced in Montana, making it easier for people to navigate snowy terrains for work and recreation.

28. Elk River Books: Located in Livingston, Elk River Books is a renowned independent bookstore that hosts literary events and fosters a vibrant community of readers and writers.

29. Grizzly Bears: Montana is home to a significant population of grizzly bears, particularly in Glacier National Park and the Northern Continental Divide Ecosystem. Efforts to conserve and manage these majestic animals are ongoing.

30. The Copper Boom: Butte's Riches

The Copper Boom in Butte, Montana, was a transformative period in American history, turning a small mining town into one of the world's largest producers of copper. This boom began in the late 19th century and continued into the early 20th century, earning Butte the nickname "The Richest Hill on Earth."

Butte's mining history started with gold and silver, but it was the discovery of vast copper deposits that truly changed the town's fortunes. Copper was in high demand due to the rise of electricity and telecommunication. As the Industrial Revolution gained momentum, copper became essential for wiring and electrical infrastructure.

In 1881, entrepreneur Marcus Daly opened the Anaconda Copper Mine, which quickly became one of the largest and most productive mines in the world. The success of the Anaconda mine attracted workers and businesses from all over, creating a bustling and diverse community. Butte's population swelled, and the town became a vibrant center of innovation and industry.

The copper industry in Butte was characterized by both immense wealth and significant challenges. The mining process was dangerous, with workers facing hazardous conditions underground. Despite these risks, the opportunity for employment and prosperity drew many immigrants, particularly from Ireland, who contributed to Butte's rich cultural tapestry.

The wealth generated from copper mining had a lasting impact on Montana's economy and infrastructure. It funded public works, education, and development across the state. However, the environmental consequences of mining, such as pollution and land degradation, have left a complex legacy that continues to be addressed today.

Butte remains a symbol of industrial might and the pioneering spirit. The town's history is celebrated at the World Museum of Mining, where visitors can explore the legacy of the Copper Boom and its influence on American industry and culture.

31. Bighorn Canyon: Straddling the Montana-Wyoming border, Bighorn Canyon National Recreation Area offers dramatic canyon landscapes, boating, hiking, and wildlife viewing.

32. Miracle of America Museum: Located in Polson, this eclectic museum houses a vast collection of Americana, including vintage vehicles, military artifacts, and quirky inventions.

33. Ousel Falls: A beautiful waterfall near Big Sky, Ousel Falls is accessible via a scenic hiking trail and is a popular spot for picnicking and photography.

34. Native American Tribes of Montana: A Rich Cultural Heritage

Montana is home to several Native American tribes, each with its own unique culture, history, and traditions. The state recognizes twelve tribes across seven reservations, reflecting a rich tapestry of indigenous heritage. These tribes include the Blackfeet, Crow, Salish and Kootenai, Northern Cheyenne, Assiniboine and Sioux, Chippewa Cree, Gros Ventre, and Little Shell Chippewa.

The Blackfeet Nation, located near Glacier National Park, is known for its strong warrior tradition and rich cultural practices, including elaborate ceremonies and storytelling. The Crow Tribe, residing in south-central Montana, has a history deeply tied to the vast plains and their renowned horse culture. The Salish and Kootenai Tribes, based on the Flathead Reservation, have a legacy of environmental stewardship and intricate beadwork and basketry.

The Northern Cheyenne Tribe, with a reservation in southeastern Montana, is celebrated for its resilience and powerful oral traditions. The Assiniboine and Sioux Tribes share the Fort Peck Reservation in northeastern Montana, blending their distinct heritages in a unified community. The Chippewa Cree Tribe, residing on the Rocky Boy's Reservation, is known for its vibrant powwows and traditional music.

The Gros Ventre (A'aninin) people, part of the Fort Belknap Reservation, are recognized for their skilled craftsmanship and profound spiritual beliefs. The Little Shell Chippewa Tribe, recently federally recognized, preserves a rich cultural legacy despite not having a designated reservation.

These tribes contribute significantly to Montana's cultural and social fabric. They hold annual powwows and cultural events that attract visitors from across the state and beyond, offering a glimpse into their vibrant traditions and way of life. Efforts to preserve and revitalize Native languages, arts, and cultural practices are ongoing, ensuring that their rich heritage continues to thrive.

35. Portable Electric Fence: The invention of the portable electric fence in Montana revolutionized livestock management by allowing ranchers to easily and efficiently contain and move their animals.

36. Fly-Fishing Innovations: Montana's rivers and streams have made it a hub for fly-fishing innovations, including the development of new fly-tying techniques and equipment that are now used worldwide.

37. Vertical Log Cabin: Montana settlers perfected the construction of vertical log cabins, which were easier to build and more durable than traditional horizontal log structures.

38. Jack Horner: Renowned paleontologist Jack Horner, who inspired the character of Dr. Alan Grant in the "Jurassic Park" series, conducted much of his groundbreaking research on dinosaur fossils in Montana.

39. The Stinger Spike System: Enhancing Law Enforcement Safety

The Stinger Spike System is a revolutionary tool developed to enhance the safety and effectiveness of law enforcement during high-speed vehicle pursuits. Invented in Montana, this system has become an essential part of police work worldwide. It was designed to stop fleeing vehicles quickly and safely by puncturing their tires, leading to a controlled and gradual deflation.

The system consists of a portable device that deploys a series of hollow spikes across the roadway. When a vehicle runs over the spikes, the hollow design allows air to escape from the tires in a controlled manner, reducing the risk of a blowout and enabling the driver to bring the vehicle to a safe stop. The Stinger Spike System can be quickly deployed and retracted, minimizing the risk to both officers and other road users.

The development of the Stinger Spike System addressed a critical need for safer methods of ending dangerous high-speed chases. Traditional methods, such as roadblocks and ramming, often posed significant risks to both law enforcement officers and the public. The Stinger system provides a non-lethal, effective alternative, helping to reduce injuries and fatalities during pursuits.

Since its introduction, the Stinger Spike System has been adopted by law enforcement agencies across the globe. Its success has led to the development of various models and improvements, ensuring it remains a vital tool in modern policing. The system's design and effectiveness have been recognized with numerous awards, highlighting its importance in enhancing public safety.

Montana's contribution to law enforcement technology through the Stinger Spike System exemplifies the state's innovative spirit and commitment to safety. It stands as a testament to the ingenuity and problem-solving abilities of Montanans, making a significant impact on public safety worldwide.

40. Fort Benton: Established in 1846, Fort Benton is one of the oldest continuously inhabited settlements in Montana. It was an important fur trading post and a hub for steamboat traffic.

41. Women's Suffrage: Montana granted women the right to vote in 1914, six years before the 19th Amendment was ratified, reflecting the state's progressive stance on women's rights.

42. Beartooth Highway: This scenic highway, which reaches elevations of nearly 11,000 feet, offers breathtaking views and access to the Beartooth Mountains, one of the highest roads in North America.

43. The Great Fire of 1910: A Historic Inferno

The Great Fire of 1910, also known as the Big Burn, was one of the most devastating wildfires in American history. It raged across northeastern Washington, northern Idaho, and western Montana, burning approximately three million acres of forest over two terrifying days in August 1910. The firestorm left a lasting legacy on wildfire management and forest conservation.

The summer of 1910 was exceptionally dry, with record-high temperatures and scant rainfall. These conditions, combined with strong winds, created the perfect environment for wildfires. On August 20 and 21, hurricane-force winds whipped small, scattered fires into a massive inferno that consumed everything in its path. The fire's intensity was so great that it created its own weather system, generating firestorms and tornadoes of flame.

The Great Fire claimed the lives of 87 people, including 78 firefighters, and devastated entire communities. The towns of Wallace, Idaho, and Avery, Montana, were nearly destroyed. The heroism of the firefighters, particularly the legendary "Pulaski's Tunnel" incident, where Ranger Ed Pulaski saved most of his 45-man crew by sheltering them in a mine tunnel, is remembered as a poignant example of bravery and sacrifice.

The fire's aftermath had a profound impact on the U.S. Forest Service and the nation's approach to wildfire management. It led to significant changes in firefighting techniques, forest management policies, and the establishment of the "10 a.m. policy," which aimed to control all wildfires by 10 a.m. the following day. The tragedy also highlighted the need for better resources and training for firefighters.

Today, the Great Fire of 1910 is a crucial chapter in the history of American forestry and firefighting. It underscores the importance of preparedness, effective management, and the relentless spirit of those who risk their lives to protect our forests and communities.

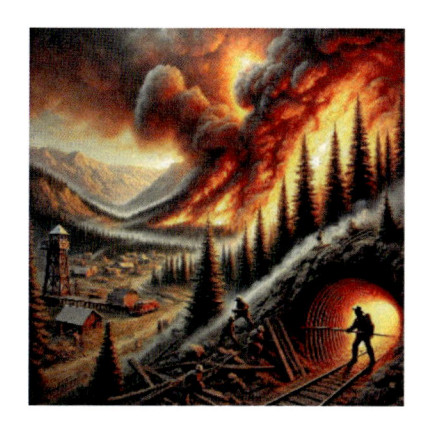

44. Granite Peak: The highest point in Montana, Granite Peak stands at 12,807 feet.

45. The Badlands: Located in eastern Montana, the badlands feature rugged, eroded landscapes and colorful rock formations, creating a unique and dramatic terrain.

46. Bitterroot Scottish Irish Festival: This festival in Hamilton celebrates the Scottish and Irish heritage of many Montanans with traditional music, dance, and Highland games.

47. The Bob Marshall Wilderness: A Pristine Natural Haven

The Bob Marshall Wilderness, located in western Montana, is one of the largest and most pristine wilderness areas in the United States. Spanning over 1.5 million acres, it is part of the larger 5.4 million-acre Bob Marshall Wilderness Complex, which also includes the Great Bear Wilderness and the Scapegoat Wilderness. Named after the influential wilderness advocate Bob Marshall, this vast expanse of wild land is renowned for its rugged beauty, diverse ecosystems, and abundant wildlife.

Bob Marshall, a forester, writer, and co-founder of The Wilderness Society, was a passionate advocate for preserving wild places. His vision and tireless efforts led to the establishment of the wilderness area that now bears his name. The Bob Marshall Wilderness was designated as part of the National Wilderness Preservation System in 1964, ensuring its protection from development and motorized use.

The wilderness area is characterized by its dramatic landscapes, including towering peaks, deep valleys, and dense forests. It is home to the Continental Divide, which runs through the heart of the wilderness, and features significant landmarks such as the Chinese Wall, a 1,000-foot-high escarpment that stretches for miles. The wilderness is also crisscrossed by numerous rivers and streams, providing critical habitat for fish and other aquatic species.

Visitors to the Bob Marshall Wilderness can experience a true sense of solitude and connection with nature. Hiking, horseback riding, and backcountry camping are popular activities, offering opportunities to explore the area's remote beauty. The wilderness is also a haven for wildlife, including grizzly bears, wolves, elk, and mountain goats, making it a prime destination for wildlife enthusiasts.

The Bob Marshall Wilderness stands as a testament to the enduring value of wilderness preservation. It serves as a refuge for both wildlife and people, offering a glimpse into the natural world as it existed before human development. The legacy of Bob Marshall and his commitment to conservation continues to inspire efforts to protect wild places for future generations.

48. Agriculture: Agriculture is a cornerstone of Montana's economy, with the state being a leading producer of wheat, barley, and beef cattle. Ranching and farming are vital to many rural communities.

49. Renewable Energy: Montana has vast potential for renewable energy, including wind, solar, and hydroelectric power. The state is investing in expanding its renewable energy infrastructure.

50. Geographical Location: Montana is located in the northwestern region of the United States. It is bordered by several states and Canadian provinces, giving it a unique geographical position. To the north, Montana shares a lengthy border with the Canadian provinces of British Columbia, Alberta, and Saskatchewan. To the east, it is bordered by North Dakota and South Dakota. Wyoming lies to the south, and Idaho forms the state's western boundary.

Montana is the fourth-largest state in the U.S. by area, encompassing diverse landscapes that range from the rugged Rocky Mountains in the west to the expansive Great Plains in the east. The Continental Divide runs through the western part of the state, creating distinct climate and ecological zones. Major rivers, such as the Missouri River and the Yellowstone River, flow through Montana, providing critical water resources and supporting rich ecosystems.

The state's major cities include Helena, the capital, located in the west-central part of the state; Billings, the largest city, situated in the south-central region; and Missoula and Bozeman, both key cultural and educational hubs nestled in the Rocky Mountains. Montana's geographical diversity includes numerous national parks and wilderness areas, such as Glacier National Park in the northwest and part of Yellowstone National Park in the southern region.

Montana's location, with its blend of mountainous terrain, rolling plains, and significant water bodies, makes it a state of stunning natural beauty and varied ecological environments.

02

NEBRASKA

1. Chimney Rock: A Landmark of the Oregon Trail

Brule clay interlayered with volcanic ash and Arikaree sandstone. Its unique shape has intrigued and inspired travelers for centuries. To the pioneers heading west, it signified progress on their arduous journey, marking the end of the plains and the beginning of the more challenging Rocky Mountains.

The sight of Chimney Rock was often met with relief and awe. Pioneer diaries and journals are filled with references to the landmark, describing it as a beacon of hope and a symbol of the vast, untamed wilderness of the American frontier. The rock also held spiritual significance for Native American tribes, including the

Lakota and Cheyenne, who inhabited the region long before the arrival of settlers.

Today, Chimney Rock is preserved as part of the Chimney Rock National Historic Site, managed by the Nebraska State Historical Society. Visitors can explore the visitor center, which features exhibits on the history of westward expansion, the natural history of the region, and the significance of Chimney Rock. The site offers a glimpse into the challenges and triumphs of the pioneers who helped shape the United States.

Chimney Rock stands as an enduring symbol of the American West, capturing the imagination of all who behold it.

2. Platte River: The Platte River runs across Nebraska and is a significant waterway for irrigation and wildlife.

3. Great Plains: Nebraska is part of the Great Plains, featuring vast prairies and grasslands.

4. Reuben Sandwich: Allegedly invented in Omaha, this sandwich features corned beef, Swiss cheese, sauerkraut, and Russian dressing.

5. The Trans-Mississippi Exposition of 1898: Showcasing the West

The Trans-Mississippi Exposition of 1898, held in Omaha, Nebraska, was a grand event designed to highlight the achievements and potential of the western United States. Often referred to as the "Omaha Exposition," this world's fair was inspired by the success of the 1893 World's Columbian Exposition in Chicago and aimed to promote economic development and cultural exchange in the western territories.

The exposition opened on June 1, 1898, and ran until November 1, attracting over 2.6 million visitors from across the country and the world. The event covered 184 acres in North Omaha, featuring more than 100 grand buildings, many designed in the neoclassical style and adorned with intricate sculptures and decorations. These structures, constructed from plaster and wood, created a temporary but awe-inspiring "White City."

Exhibits at the Trans-Mississippi Exposition showcased advancements in agriculture, industry, and technology, emphasizing the growth and opportunities in the western United States. Key highlights included displays of the latest farming equipment, innovative manufacturing techniques, and cultural exhibits from various states and territories. The exposition also featured attractions such as amusement rides, theatrical performances, and ethnographic displays, providing entertainment and education for visitors.

One of the most significant aspects of the exposition was its role in promoting Omaha as a burgeoning urban center. The event helped establish the city's reputation as a hub of commerce and innovation, attracting new businesses and residents. The exposition also had a lasting impact on the local community, leading to improvements in infrastructure and the development of public spaces.

Today, the legacy of the Trans-Mississippi Exposition is commemorated in Omaha through various historical markers and the Trans-Mississippi and International Exposition Historical Society. The event remains a proud moment in Nebraska's history, symbolizing the state's spirit of progress and its pivotal role in the development of the American West.

6. Nebraska Territory: Established in 1854, the Nebraska Territory was a significant area for westward expansion and settlement.

7. Statehood: Nebraska joined the Union in 1867 (Mar. 1) and was the 37th state to do so.

8. Carhenge: A quirky replica of Stonehenge made from vintage cars near Alliance.

9. Nebraska National Forest: The largest hand-planted forest in the United States.

10. Nebraska's World War II POW Camps: A Hidden History

During World War II, Nebraska played a crucial yet often overlooked role in housing German and Italian prisoners of war (POWs). The state hosted several POW camps, with the largest being located at Fort Robinson, Camp Atlanta, and Camp Scottsbluff. These camps were established to house the growing number of Axis soldiers captured by Allied forces, providing a secure and humane environment far from the battlefronts.

The largest and most significant camp was at Fort Robinson, which housed up to 3,000 German soldiers. The POWs at Fort Robinson and other camps were put to work in various capacities, including agricultural labor, which was vital to the local economy due to the labor shortage caused by the war. They worked on farms, in canneries, and on construction projects, helping to sustain food production and infrastructure development.

Life in the Nebraska POW camps was generally considered fair and humane, adhering to the standards set by the Geneva Convention. The prisoners were provided with adequate food, medical care, and recreational activities. They had opportunities to learn English, attend classes, and participate in sports, which helped alleviate the monotony and stress of internment. Many former POWs later spoke positively about their treatment and experiences in Nebraska.

The presence of the POW camps had a lasting impact on the local communities. It fostered cultural exchanges and, in some cases, led to lasting friendships between the prisoners and local residents. After the war, some former POWs even chose to return to Nebraska, drawn by the hospitality and opportunities they experienced during their internment.

Today, the history of Nebraska's POW camps is preserved through museums and historical markers. Fort Robinson State Park, in particular, offers exhibits and tours that provide insights into this unique chapter of the state's history, ensuring that the contributions and experiences of the POWs are remembered.

11. Sandhills: Covering over a quarter of the state, the Sandhills are the largest sand dune formation in the Western Hemisphere.

12. Oregon Trail: A significant portion of the Oregon Trail runs through Nebraska.

13. College World Series: Omaha hosts the annual NCAA Division I Baseball Championship.

14. The Invention of Frozen Food Packaging: A Revolution in Food Preservation

The invention of frozen food packaging revolutionized the way we preserve and consume food, and much of this innovation can be traced back to the research conducted in Nebraska. Clarence Birdseye, often credited as the father of the frozen food industry, developed methods for quick-freezing food that would retain its flavor and nutritional value. While Birdseye himself did much of his early work in the Northeastern United States, Nebraska played a significant role in the advancement and commercialization of frozen food packaging.

In the 1920s and 1930s, food scientists and agricultural researchers in Nebraska worked on refining Birdseye's techniques and developing practical packaging solutions that would protect the food during freezing and storage. The University of Nebraska-Lincoln was at the forefront of this research, contributing to the development of durable and efficient packaging materials that could withstand the rigors of the freezing process and prevent freezer burn.

The breakthrough came with the creation of moisture-proof cellophane and other plastic-based materials that provided an effective barrier against air and moisture. This advancement ensured that frozen foods could be stored for extended periods without significant loss of quality. These packaging innovations were crucial for the mass production and distribution of frozen foods, making them accessible to households across the country.

The impact of frozen food packaging on the food industry was profound. It enabled the year-round availability of seasonal foods, reduced food waste, and made meal preparation more convenient. The ability to preserve food at peak freshness also contributed to better nutrition and variety in diets.

Today, the frozen food industry continues to thrive, thanks in part to the pioneering research conducted in Nebraska. The state's contributions to food science and technology have left an indelible mark on the way we eat and enjoy food, underscoring the importance of innovation in everyday life.

15. Husker Harvest Days: One of the largest farm shows in the nation, held annually near Grand Island, showcasing agricultural innovations.

16. Joan Micklin Silver: The groundbreaking filmmaker was born in Omaha.

17. L. Ron Hubbard: The founder of Scientology was born in Tilden, Nebraska.

18. Cabela's: Founded in Chappell, Nebraska, this outdoor recreation retail company is now headquartered in Sidney.

19. The Vise-Grip: A Handy Invention from Nebraska

The Vise-Grip, an essential tool for countless craftsmen and DIY enthusiasts, was invented by a Nebraska blacksmith named William Petersen. In 1924, Petersen, who lived in the small town of De Witt, Nebraska, was searching for a way to improve the clamping and gripping of materials in his work. His innovative solution was a set of locking pliers that could hold objects firmly in place, providing a third hand to assist with various tasks.

Petersen's original design featured an adjustable mechanism that allowed the user to clamp objects with a consistent and secure grip. The locking feature set the Vise-Grip apart from other pliers, making it a versatile tool for a wide range of applications. From automotive repairs to woodworking and metalworking, the Vise-Grip quickly became an indispensable tool in workshops around the world.

Recognizing the potential of his invention, Petersen founded the Petersen Manufacturing Company in De Witt, where he began mass-producing the Vise-Grip. The company remained family-owned and operated for several decades, contributing to the local economy and providing jobs for the community. The Vise-Grip's success also helped put De Witt on the map, earning it the nickname "The Home of the Vise-Grip."

Over the years, the design of the Vise-Grip has evolved, incorporating new materials and ergonomic improvements. Despite these changes, the core functionality of the tool remains true to Petersen's original vision. Today, the Vise-Grip is manufactured by Irwin Tools, which acquired the Petersen Manufacturing Company in 1993. The tool continues to be a favorite among professionals and hobbyists alike, a testament to the enduring legacy of Petersen's ingenuity.

20. Swedish Heritage: Lindsborg and other communities celebrate their Swedish heritage with festivals and cultural events.

21. German-American Society: Omaha's German-American Society hosts cultural events celebrating German traditions and heritage.

22. Czech Festivals: Nebraska celebrates its Czech heritage with festivals featuring traditional music, dance, and food.

23. Pioneer Heritage: Many towns in Nebraska celebrate their pioneer heritage with festivals and museums dedicated to the state's early settlers.

24. The Union Pacific Railroad: Building America

The Union Pacific Railroad, headquartered in Omaha, Nebraska, is a vital part of American history and has played a significant role in shaping the nation's transportation infrastructure. Founded in 1862 under the Pacific Railway Act, the Union Pacific was created to build a transcontinental railroad that would connect the eastern United States with the Pacific coast. This ambitious project was crucial for economic growth, national unity, and westward expansion.

Construction of the Union Pacific Railroad began in Omaha, Nebraska, in 1863. The company faced numerous challenges, including difficult terrain, harsh weather conditions, and conflicts with Native American tribes. Despite these obstacles, the Union Pacific made remarkable progress, thanks to the labor of thousands of workers, including many Irish immigrants and Civil War veterans.

The completion of the transcontinental railroad was achieved on May 10, 1869, when the Union Pacific tracks met those of the Central Pacific Railroad at Promontory Summit in Utah. This historic event was marked by the driving of the Golden Spike, symbolizing the unification of the country from coast to coast. The railroad significantly reduced travel time across the continent, facilitated commerce, and contributed to the rapid settlement and development of the western United States.

Today, the Union Pacific Railroad continues to be a major freight carrier, operating over 32,000 miles of track across 23 states. It plays a crucial role in transporting goods, including agricultural products, industrial materials, and consumer goods, supporting the national economy and providing vital links between communities.

The Union Pacific Railroad's legacy is celebrated in Omaha at the Union Pacific Railroad Museum, which offers exhibits on the company's history, the challenges of building the transcontinental railroad, and the impact of rail transportation on American society.

25. Johnny Carson: The legendary late-night talk show host was born in Corning, Iowa, and grew up in Norfolk, Nebraska.

26. The Nebraska State Capitol: An Architectural Masterpiece

The Nebraska State Capitol in Lincoln is not just the seat of government; it is an architectural masterpiece and a symbol of the state's rich history and cultural heritage. Designed by renowned architect Bertram Grosvenor Goodhue, the capitol building is unique for its towering structure and elegant blend of classical and modern design elements.

Construction of the current state capitol began in 1922 and was completed in 1932. Standing at 400 feet tall, the building is one of the few state capitols in the United States to have a central tower. This tower, known as the "Tower on the Plains," is crowned by a bronze statue of a farmer sowing grain, symbolizing Nebraska's agricultural roots and its forward-looking spirit.

The exterior of the building is clad in Indiana limestone, and its walls are adorned with intricate carvings and friezes that depict significant events and themes from Nebraska's history. Inside, the capitol is just as impressive, featuring stunning mosaics, murals, and marble floors. The interior artwork tells the story of the state's development, from its indigenous peoples and pioneers to its agricultural and industrial achievements.

The Nebraska State Capitol is also notable for its innovative structural design. It was one of the first state capitols to be constructed with a steel frame, which provides both strength and flexibility, allowing the building to withstand the region's strong winds and occasional earthquakes.

Today, the Nebraska State Capitol is not only a functioning seat of government but also a popular tourist attraction. Visitors can take guided tours to learn about the building's history, architecture, and the state's legislative process. The capitol's observation deck offers breathtaking views of Lincoln and the surrounding plains, providing a unique perspective on the state's landscape.

27. TV Dinner: The concept of the TV dinner was popularized by Omaha-based Swanson in the 1950s, revolutionizing convenience food.

28. University of Nebraska-Lincoln: The state's largest and oldest university, founded in 1869.

29. Smith Falls: The tallest waterfall in Nebraska, located in Smith Falls State Park.

30. CliffsNotes: A Lifesaver for Students

CliffsNotes, a brand synonymous with academic support and literary analysis, was created by Clifton Hillegass in Lincoln, Nebraska. The story of CliffsNotes began in 1958 when Hillegass, who was working for a publishing company, met Jack Cole, the owner of a Canadian company that published study guides for Shakespeare plays. Inspired by Cole's idea, Hillegass decided to create similar guides for American students, starting with literature.

Hillegass launched CliffsNotes with 16 Shakespeare titles, investing $4,000 of his own money to print the first batch. The guides quickly gained popularity for their concise summaries, character analyses, and insightful commentaries, making complex literary works more accessible to students. The black and yellow covers of CliffsNotes soon became a familiar sight on college campuses across the United States.

CliffsNotes filled a critical need by helping students understand and engage with challenging texts. Each guide provided an overview of the book's plot, themes, and characters, along with critical interpretations that encouraged deeper analysis. While some educators were initially skeptical, many recognized the value of CliffsNotes as a supplementary resource that could enhance students' comprehension and foster a love for reading.

Over the years, CliffsNotes expanded beyond literature to include a wide range of subjects, such as history, science, and math. The brand continued to evolve with the times, embracing digital formats and online resources to reach a broader audience. Today,

CliffsNotes remains a trusted name in educational publishing, helping millions of students worldwide succeed academically.

Clifton Hillegass's vision and entrepreneurial spirit transformed a simple idea into a lasting educational tool. CliffsNotes not only supported countless students in their studies but also contributed to a broader understanding and appreciation of literature and learning.

31. Tom Osborne: Legendary football coach and politician, Osborne coached the Nebraska Cornhuskers to multiple national championships.

32. Toadstool Geologic Park: Known for its unique rock formations and fossil beds.

33. Rowe Sanctuary: A key stopover site for Sandhill Cranes during their migration.

34. The Car Anti-Theft Device: George Long's Innovative Solution

In 1923, George Long of Omaha, Nebraska, patented a revolutionary car anti-theft device that significantly improved vehicle security. During the early 20th century, car theft was a growing concern as automobiles became more common. Long's invention provided an effective deterrent against theft, offering car owners peace of mind.

Long's anti-theft device was a mechanical system that locked the steering wheel and ignition, making it nearly impossible for thieves to start or drive the car without the proper key. This innovation addressed the limitations of earlier security measures, which were often easy to bypass. Long's design incorporated a lock mechanism directly into the vehicle's steering column and ignition switch, ensuring that both components were securely immobilized when the device was activated.

The invention quickly gained popularity among car owners and manufacturers. It was relatively simple to install and use, providing a reliable and cost-effective solution to a widespread problem. Long's device set the standard for vehicle security at the time and paved the way for future advancements in automotive safety.

Long's contribution to car security had a lasting impact on the automotive industry. It highlighted the importance of integrating safety features into vehicle design and spurred further innovations in car theft prevention. Today, modern vehicles come equipped with advanced security systems, including electronic immobilizers and GPS tracking, building on the principles established by Long's early work.

George Long's ingenuity and foresight helped make car ownership safer and more secure. His anti-theft device not only protected vehicles but also contributed to a broader culture of innovation and safety in the automotive industry, ensuring that car owners could enjoy their vehicles with greater confidence.

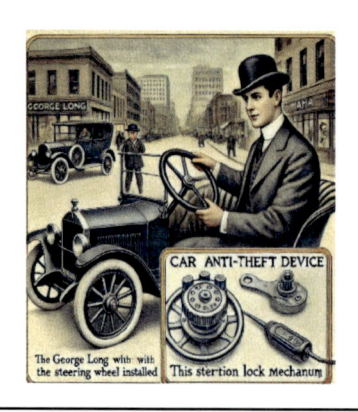

35. Ashfall Fossil Beds: A unique site preserving the remains of prehistoric animals that died in a volcanic ashfall.

36. Ruth Etting: The famous singer and actress of the 1920s and 1930s was born in David City, Nebraska.

37. Indian Cave State Park: Features prehistoric petroglyphs and beautiful hiking trails.

38. Nick Nolte: The Academy Award-nominated actor was born in Omaha.

39. Kool-Aid: Nebraska's Sweet Invention

Kool-Aid, the iconic powdered drink mix that has delighted generations, was invented in 1927 by Edwin Perkins in Hastings, Nebraska. Perkins was an innovative entrepreneur with a keen interest in creating new products. He initially started with a liquid concentrate called Fruit Smack, which he sold in glass bottles. However, the fragility and shipping costs of the bottles led him to seek a more convenient solution.

Inspired by Jell-O, Perkins devised a method to dehydrate the liquid concentrate into a powdered form. This new product, which he called Kool-Ade (later changed to Kool-Aid), could be packaged in small, easy-to-ship envelopes. The powder could be mixed with water to create a refreshing, fruity beverage. This innovation not only reduced shipping costs but also increased the product's shelf life and accessibility.

Kool-Aid quickly became a hit with consumers, thanks to its affordability and convenience. Families loved the variety of flavors, which included cherry, grape, lemon-lime, orange, raspberry, and strawberry. The vibrant colors and sweet taste made it especially popular with children. Perkins' clever marketing strategies, including colorful packaging and engaging advertising campaigns, further boosted Kool-Aid's appeal.

In 1953, Perkins sold the Kool-Aid brand to General Foods (now Kraft Heinz), ensuring its continued growth and success. Today, Kool-Aid is a household name and remains a beloved beverage choice for kids and adults alike. The city of Hastings celebrates its connection to this iconic product with an annual Kool-Aid Days festival, featuring parades, games, and plenty of Kool-Aid.

Edwin Perkins' ingenuity and entrepreneurial spirit left a lasting legacy in the world of beverages. Kool-Aid's enduring popularity demonstrates the power of innovation and the ability to turn a simple idea into a timeless classic.

40. Prairie Dog Towns: Nebraska is home to numerous prairie dog colonies, which are critical to the prairie ecosystem.

41. Sandhill Crane Migration: Each year, hundreds of thousands of Sandhill Cranes migrate through Nebraska, particularly the Platte River Valley, making it one of the most significant wildlife spectacles in North America.

42. Prairie Chicken: Nebraska is a key habitat for the Greater Prairie Chicken, known for its unique mating dance.

43. The Cornhusker Car: A Nebraska Automotive Innovation

The Cornhusker Car, an early example of Nebraska's contribution to automotive innovation, was a remarkable achievement in the early 20th century. Developed in the 1910s, this unique vehicle was the brainchild of local engineers and craftsmen who aimed to create a reliable and efficient car tailored to the needs of Nebraskans.

The Cornhusker Car was designed with practicality and durability in mind, making it well-suited for the rough and varied terrains of Nebraska. It featured a robust chassis and a powerful engine that provided excellent performance on both city streets and rural roads. The car's design incorporated elements that were advanced for its time, such as a more comfortable suspension system and improved fuel efficiency.

One of the most notable aspects of the Cornhusker Car was its emphasis on local manufacturing. The vehicle was produced using materials sourced from Nebraska and assembled by local workers, fostering a sense of pride and community involvement. This focus on local production helped support the state's economy and showcased Nebraska's potential as a center for industrial innovation.

Although the Cornhusker Car was not produced in large quantities, it left a significant impact on the region. It demonstrated the feasibility of building quality automobiles outside of the established automotive hubs like Detroit. The car also paved the way for future innovations in vehicle design and manufacturing within the state.

Today, the legacy of the Cornhusker Car is remembered as a symbol of Nebraska's pioneering spirit and commitment to innovation. It serves as an inspiring example of what can be achieved through collaboration, creativity, and a strong sense of community.

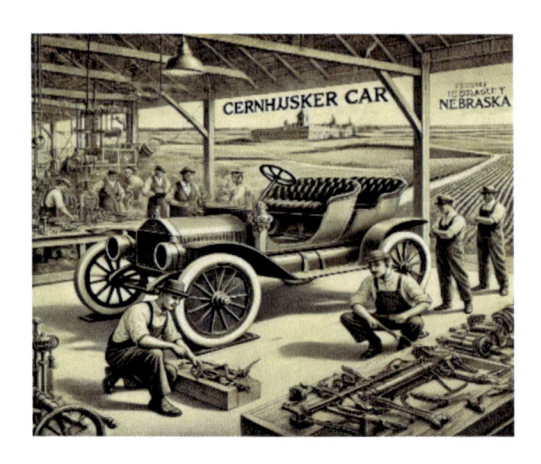

44. Ogallala Aquifer: One of the largest aquifers in the world, it provides essential water for agriculture and communities in Nebraska.

45. Buffalo Herds: Efforts to reintroduce and conserve buffalo have been successful in parts of Nebraska, particularly in state parks and wildlife refuges.

46. Omaha Race Riot of 1919: A significant and tragic event in Nebraska's history, reflecting racial tensions and leading to substantial social change.

47. Arbor Day: Planting the Seeds of Conservation

Arbor Day, a holiday dedicated to planting and caring for trees, has its roots in Nebraska, thanks to the vision of J. Sterling Morton. Morton, a journalist and politician, moved to Nebraska City, Nebraska, in 1854. He was passionate about nature and recognized the need for trees in the largely treeless plains of Nebraska. Trees, he believed, would provide much-needed windbreaks, fuel, building materials, and shade, enhancing both the environment and quality of life.

Morton's advocacy for tree planting culminated in the establishment of the first Arbor Day on April 10, 1872. The day was a resounding success, with Nebraskans planting over one million trees. Encouraged by this initial success, Morton continued to promote Arbor Day, and by 1885, it was declared a legal holiday in Nebraska, celebrated on April 22, Morton's birthday.

The idea of Arbor Day quickly spread beyond Nebraska. States across the country adopted the holiday, each celebrating it at different times depending on the best tree-planting season for their region. The concept even gained international appeal, with many countries around the world establishing their own Arbor Day celebrations.

Arbor Day's significance lies not just in tree planting but also in fostering a broader environmental consciousness. The holiday encourages individuals and communities to take proactive steps in conserving and enhancing their local environments. Schools, civic groups, and governments participate in Arbor Day activities, planting trees and educating people about the importance of forests.

In Nebraska, the Arbor Day Foundation, founded in 1972, continues Morton's legacy by promoting tree planting and environmental stewardship on a global scale. The foundation's programs, such as the "Tree City USA" initiative, support urban forestry efforts, and its tree-planting campaigns help reforest areas affected by natural disasters.

Arbor Day remains a powerful reminder of the impact one person's vision can have on the world. J. Sterling Morton's commitment to tree planting has left an enduring legacy, inspiring generations to appreciate and protect our natural environment.

48. Blizzard of 1888: Also known as the Schoolhouse Blizzard, this severe storm resulted in numerous deaths and highlighted the harsh conditions of pioneer life.

49. Battle of Blue Water: A significant conflict between the U.S. Army and the Lakota Sioux in 1855, occurring near present-day Lewellen.

50. Geographical Location: Nebraska is located in the central part of the United States, within the Great Plains region. It is bordered by six states: South Dakota to the north, Iowa to the east, Missouri to the southeast, Kansas to the south, Colorado to the southwest, and Wyoming to the west. The Missouri River forms much of Nebraska's eastern boundary with Iowa and Missouri.

Nebraska's landscape is characterized by diverse geographical features. The eastern part of the state is known for its fertile soil and rolling hills, making it ideal for agriculture. This region is part of the Dissected Till Plains. The central and western parts of Nebraska are dominated by the vast, treeless prairies of the Great Plains, with the Sandhills, a large area of mixed-grass prairie on dunes, located in the north-central part of the state. The Panhandle, in the far western region, features more rugged terrain with bluffs and rock formations.

Major rivers in Nebraska include the Platte River, which runs across the state from west to east, and the Niobrara River in the north. These waterways are crucial for irrigation and agriculture. Nebraska's climate varies from humid continental in the east to semi-arid in the west, with hot summers and cold winters.

Nebraska's major cities include Omaha, the largest city, situated along the Missouri River in the eastern part of the state, and Lincoln, the state capital, located slightly to the southwest of Omaha. Other notable cities include Grand Island, Kearney, and Scottsbluff.

Overall, Nebraska's central location and diverse landscapes play a significant role in its agricultural productivity and cultural heritage.

03

NEVADA

1. Nevada's Statehood Telegram

In the throes of the Civil War, President Abraham Lincoln sought to bolster his support base by admitting Nevada as a state, crucial for securing votes for his re-election and the passage of the 13th Amendment to abolish slavery. However, with time running out before the election, Nevada faced a logistical challenge. The state needed to submit its constitution to Washington, D.C., but with no reliable means of quickly transporting the document over the vast distances, an innovative solution was required.

Governor James W. Nye and his colleagues decided to send the constitution via telegraph, an unprecedented move at the time. On October 26, 1864, the 16,543-word document began its transmission from Carson City. The task took two days, as operators meticulously tapped out each word, ensuring accuracy in the face of immense pressure. This transmission, costing over $3,000, is said to be the longest and most expensive telegram ever sent.

This feat of communication and technological prowess ensured that Nevada's statehood was secured just days before the election. On October 31, 1864, President Lincoln proclaimed Nevada the 36th state, with its telegraphed constitution cementing its place in history. Nevada Day is celebrated every October 31, marking the state's admission to the Union.

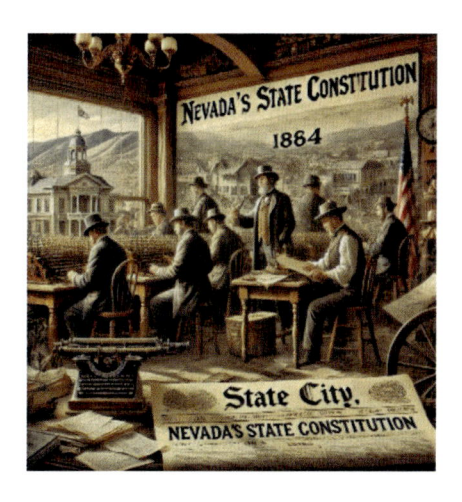

2. Mormon Settlers: The first non-native settlers in the Las Vegas Valley were Mormon missionaries in 1855.

3. Area 51: Established in 1955, this secretive military base has been the subject of many UFO conspiracy theories.

4. Zamora Incident: In 1964, a UFO sighting by a police officer in Socorro, New Mexico, indirectly linked to Area 51 rumors.

5. Ivanpah Solar Electric Generating System

The Ivanpah Solar Electric Generating System, located in the Mojave Desert near the California-Nevada border, stands as a testament to Nevada's commitment to renewable energy. Officially opened in February 2014, Ivanpah is one of the world's largest solar thermal power plants, symbolizing a leap towards sustainable energy.

Ivanpah utilizes a vast array of 173,500 heliostats—mirrors that track the sun and focus sunlight onto boilers atop three 459-foot tall towers. This concentrated sunlight heats the boilers to produce steam, which then drives turbines to generate electricity. With a capacity of 392 megawatts, Ivanpah powers approximately 140,000 homes, reducing carbon emissions by over 400,000 tons annually.

The project, a collaboration between NRG Energy, BrightSource Energy, and Google, represents a significant investment in green technology. It also highlights the challenges and innovations in harnessing solar power, from overcoming environmental concerns to optimizing energy output.

Ivanpah's success showcases Nevada's potential as a leader in renewable energy, aligning with global efforts to combat climate change. The facility stands not only as an engineering marvel but also as a beacon of hope for a sustainable future.

6. First Nevada Governor: Henry Blasdel was the first governor after statehood.

7. Economic Diversification: Nevada has worked to diversify its economy beyond gaming and mining, including tech and renewable energy sectors.

8. Howard Hughes: The reclusive billionaire made significant investments in Las Vegas casinos in the 1960s.

9. Las Vegas Residency: Celebrities like Elvis Presley and Frank Sinatra had iconic residencies in Las Vegas.

10. Las Vegas Atomic Bomb Tours

During the 1950s, the Cold War era ushered in an unlikely and surreal chapter in American history: atomic bomb tourism in Las Vegas. At the height of nuclear testing at the Nevada Test Site, located just 65 miles northwest of the city, the spectacle of atomic explosions became a curious attraction.

Las Vegas capitalized on its proximity to the test site, turning nuclear detonations into a form of entertainment. Hotels and casinos advertised "bomb-watching" events, with prime viewing spots on their rooftops. Tourists and residents alike would gather, often with cocktails in hand, to witness the awe-inspiring mushroom clouds that lit up the desert sky. The detonations, conducted in the early morning, provided an eerie juxtaposition to the city's vibrant nightlife.

The atomic blasts were seen as a symbol of American strength and technological prowess during a time of intense geopolitical tension. Hotels such as the Desert Inn and the Sands offered special "Dawn Bomb Parties," where guests could watch the explosions from the comfort of their hotel lounges or swimming pools. This bizarre form of tourism brought a unique, if somewhat macabre, boost to the Las Vegas economy.

However, the environmental and health impacts of the testing were significant and long-lasting. The practice of nuclear testing in Nevada was halted in 1992, but the legacy of those atomic bomb tours remains a fascinating and peculiar chapter in the history of Las Vegas.

11. Art Installation: The International Car Forest of the Last Church, an outdoor art installation, is located in Goldfield, Nevada.

12. The E.T. Highway: The Extraterrestrial Highway, State Route 375, is near Area 51 and is famous for UFO sightings.

13. Large State: Nevada is the seventh-largest state in the U.S. by area.

14. The Biggest Little City in the World

Reno, Nevada, proudly bears the nickname "The Biggest Little City in the World." This moniker, which encapsulates Reno's unique blend of small-town charm and big-city amenities, has been a part of the city's identity since the early 20th century.

In the 1920s, Reno began to rise as a major gambling center, even before Las Vegas became synonymous with casinos. The city's convenient divorce laws also attracted many seeking quick and easy separations, contributing to its booming economy. By the 1930s, Reno was the gambling capital of the United States.

The slogan "The Biggest Little City in the World" was first used in 1929, capturing the spirit of a city that offered the excitement and entertainment of a larger metropolis while maintaining a friendly, approachable atmosphere. This identity was further solidified with the construction of the iconic Reno Arch in 1926, which has since been relocated and updated, but continues to welcome visitors with its famous tagline.

Reno's growth continued with the development of the University of Nevada, Reno, which became a center for education and research. The city also embraced outdoor recreation, with its proximity to Lake Tahoe and the Sierra Nevada mountains offering abundant opportunities for skiing, hiking, and water sports.

Today, Reno blends its historic roots with modern attractions, including a thriving arts scene and technology sector. The nickname "The Biggest Little City in the World" remains a testament to Reno's enduring appeal and its ability to offer something for everyone, from its historic downtown to its scenic surroundings.

15. State Reptile: Nevada's state reptile is the desert tortoise.

16. State Fossil: Nevada's State Fossil is the Ichthyosaur, a large marine reptile.

17. Wildlife: Nevada has a diverse range of wildlife, including wild horses, mule deer, and mountain lions.

18. Voting Rights: Nevada was the first state to ratify the 15th Amendment, granting African American men the right to vote.

19. World's Largest Telescope Array

The Very Energetic Radiation Imaging Telescope Array System (VERITAS) is located in southern Nevada at the Fred Lawrence Whipple Observatory. This impressive array of telescopes is part of the world's largest collection of ground-based telescopes designed to study gamma rays from astronomical sources.

Established in 2007, VERITAS consists of four 12-meter diameter reflectors equipped with state-of-the-art photomultiplier tubes to detect the faint flashes of blue Cherenkov light produced when high-energy gamma rays interact with the Earth's atmosphere. This facility allows scientists to observe gamma rays emanating from supernova remnants, active galactic nuclei, and even potential sources of dark matter.

Nevada's clear, dry skies provide an optimal environment for such precise astronomical observations, minimizing atmospheric interference. The collaboration behind VERITAS includes multiple universities and research institutions, reflecting a significant international effort to advance our understanding of the universe.

The data collected by VERITAS has contributed to numerous groundbreaking discoveries, including the identification of new gamma-ray sources and insights into the most energetic processes in the cosmos. By studying gamma rays, scientists can probe environments that are otherwise inaccessible, such as the immediate vicinity of black holes and the remnants of explosive stellar events.

VERITAS represents not only a remarkable technological achievement but also demonstrates the collaborative spirit of the scientific community, pushing the boundaries of human knowledge about the universe.

20. Tax: The state has no corporate income tax.

21. Quick Weddings: Nevada is known for its liberal marriage laws, making it a popular destination for quick weddings.

22. Population: The state has a population of over 3 million people.

23. Las Vegas: Las Vegas was founded in 1905 and incorporated in 1911.

24. Red Rock Canyon National Conservation Area

Red Rock Canyon National Conservation Area, located just 17 miles west of Las Vegas, is a stunning natural wonder that showcases Nevada's diverse geological and ecological beauty. Established as Nevada's first National Conservation Area in 1990, it spans nearly 200,000 acres of pristine desert landscape.

The area is famous for its towering red sandstone peaks, some of which rise more than 3,000 feet above the valley floor. These formations, part of the larger Mojave Desert, are the result of millions of years of geological activity, including ancient sand dunes that were compressed and lithified, followed by faulting and erosion.

Red Rock Canyon is not only a geological treasure but also a haven for outdoor enthusiasts. The area offers a wide range of recreational activities, including hiking, rock climbing, horseback riding, and scenic drives. The 13-mile scenic loop drive provides breathtaking views and access to various trailheads and overlooks.

The conservation area is also home to a rich array of flora and fauna. Visitors can spot desert tortoises, bighorn sheep, and a variety of bird species. The spring and fall seasons bring vibrant wildflower blooms, adding splashes of color to the rugged landscape.

The conservation efforts at Red Rock Canyon focus on preserving its unique natural features and biodiversity. The visitor center provides educational exhibits about the area's natural history, cultural heritage, and ongoing conservation initiatives.

Red Rock Canyon stands as an example of Nevada's natural beauty and a reminder of the importance of preserving such landscapes for future generations to enjoy.

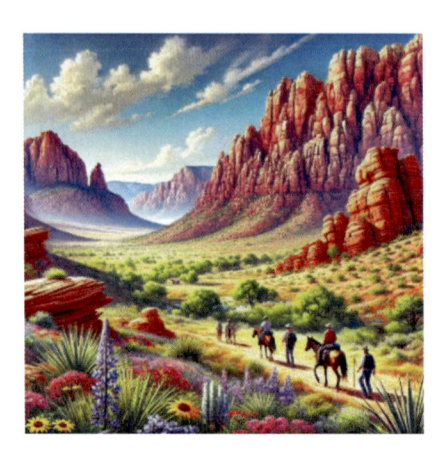

25. Native American: The state is home to several Native American tribes, including the Shoshone, Paiute, and Washoe.

26. The Loneliest Road in America:

U.S. Route 50, famously dubbed "The Loneliest Road in America" by Life magazine in July 1986, stretches across Nevada's vast, desolate landscape. This moniker, intended as a caution, ironically became a point of pride and a badge of honor for the state, attracting adventurous travelers seeking solitude and scenic beauty.

Spanning from Ely in the east to Carson City in the west, Route 50 traverses approximately 300 miles of Nevada's most remote and sparsely populated regions. The road cuts through a stunning array of landscapes, including high desert plains, rugged mountains, and ancient lakebeds. Travelers encounter a series of small towns and historic sites, each with its unique charm and history.

One of the highlights along Route 50 is the Great Basin National Park, home to the ancient Bristlecone pines and the majestic Wheeler

Peak. The park offers a stark contrast to the surrounding desert with its lush alpine environment and diverse wildlife. Another point of interest is the old mining town of Austin, a relic of Nevada's silver rush era, where remnants of the past stand frozen in time.

Despite its reputation for desolation, "The Loneliest Road" offers a sense of adventure and tranquility. Visitors receive a "Highway 50 Survival Guide" at the start of their journey, encouraging them to collect stamps from the few towns along the way. Completing the guide earns them a certificate of survival, a testament to their endurance and spirit of exploration.

The Loneliest Road in America embodies the rugged, independent spirit of Nevada, inviting travelers to disconnect from the hustle of modern life and reconnect with the raw beauty of the natural world.

27. Basque Immigrants: Basque sheepherders settled in Nevada in the 19th century, significantly contributing to the state's cultural heritage.

28. Gaming Legalization: Gambling was legalized in Nevada in 1931, transforming the state's economy.

29. Bugsy Siegel: The notorious gangster played a key role in the development of the Las Vegas Strip with the opening of the Flamingo Hotel in 1946.

30. The Mojave Desert:

The Mojave Desert, a vast and iconic desert in the southwestern United States, extends into southeastern Nevada. Known for its stark beauty and extreme conditions, the Mojave is one of the driest and hottest deserts in North America. It covers over 47,000 square miles, with significant portions in California, Arizona, and Utah, as well as Nevada.

Characterized by its unique geology and diverse ecosystems, the Mojave Desert is home to a wide array of flora and fauna. The Joshua tree, a distinctive and iconic species, is perhaps the most recognizable symbol of the Mojave. These twisted, spiky trees dominate the landscape, particularly in areas like the Joshua Tree National Park, which extends into California.

The Mojave is not only a natural wonder but also a region of great historical and cultural significance. Native American tribes, such as the Mojave, Chemehuevi, and Southern Paiute, have inhabited this harsh environment for thousands of years, adapting to its extreme conditions and thriving in its unique ecosystem. Petroglyphs and other archaeological sites throughout the desert bear witness to their ancient presence.

Modern history has also left its mark on the Mojave. Route 66, the legendary "Main Street of America," passes through the desert, offering a nostalgic journey through classic Americana. The Mojave Air and Space Port, located in California but influencing the broader region, is a hub for aerospace innovation and the development of space tourism.

In Nevada, the Mojave Desert encompasses the Las Vegas Valley, where the bright lights and bustling activity of the city provide a stark contrast to the surrounding barren landscape. The Mojave's vast expanse offers endless opportunities for exploration, from hiking and rock climbing to off-road adventures and stargazing under some of the darkest skies in the country.

The Mojave Desert is a land of extremes and contrasts, where life thrives against all odds, and history blends seamlessly with natural splendor.

31. Sagebrush Rebellion: In the late 1970s, Nevada was central to this movement against federal land control in the West.

32. Red Power Movement: The American Indian Movement held significant protests at the Nevada Test Site in the 1980s.

33. Mining Towns: Historic mining towns like Goldfield and Tonopah boomed and busted with the rise and fall of mineral discoveries.

34. Lake Tahoe

Lake Tahoe, nestled in the Sierra Nevada mountains on the border of California and Nevada, is one of the largest and most stunning alpine lakes in North America. Covering over 191 square miles, it is renowned for its crystal-clear waters and breathtaking scenery, attracting millions of visitors each year.

The lake was formed approximately two million years ago during the ice ages, and its clarity is attributed to the purity of the surrounding watershed and minimal nutrient influx. At its deepest point, Lake Tahoe plunges to 1,645 feet, making it the second deepest lake in the United States after Crater Lake in Oregon.

Lake Tahoe's history is rich with cultural and recreational significance. For thousands of years, the Washoe people lived around the lake, relying on its abundant resources. They named it "dá?aw," meaning "the lake." European-American settlers discovered the lake in the mid-19th century, and it quickly became a popular destination during the Comstock Lode silver rush.

Today, Lake Tahoe is a year-round playground for outdoor enthusiasts. In the winter, the surrounding mountains transform into world-class ski resorts, such as Heavenly, Squaw Valley, and Northstar. The summer months offer opportunities for boating, fishing, hiking, and camping. The lake's scenic beauty and recreational opportunities have made it a top destination for tourists and nature lovers alike.

Environmental preservation efforts are crucial to maintaining Lake Tahoe's pristine condition. Organizations like the Tahoe Regional Planning Agency work tirelessly to protect the lake's water quality and surrounding ecosystems. These efforts ensure that Lake Tahoe remains a natural treasure for future generations to enjoy.

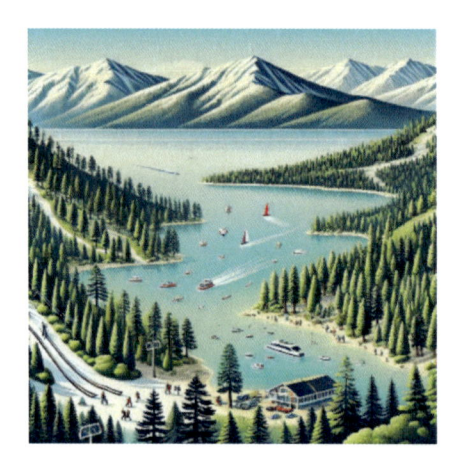

35. Pat Nixon: The First Lady, wife of President Richard Nixon, was born in Ely, Nevada.

36. Sarah Winnemucca: A Paiute author and educator, she was an advocate for Native American rights in the 19th century.

37. Railroad Completion: The Central Pacific Railroad reached Nevada in 1868, linking it to the transcontinental railroad.

38. Driverless Car Testing: Nevada was one of the first states to authorize the testing of autonomous vehicles on public roads, attracting tech companies to test their innovations.

39. Comstock Lode:

The Comstock Lode, discovered in 1859 in Virginia City, Nevada, is one of the most significant silver ore deposits in history. This discovery transformed Nevada's economy and played a pivotal role in the state's early development.

The discovery of the Comstock Lode is credited to Henry Comstock, though it was actually two miners, Peter O'Riley and Patrick McLaughlin, who stumbled upon the rich vein of silver while digging for gold. The Comstock Lode's richness soon attracted thousands of prospectors, and Virginia City quickly became a booming mining town.

The influx of wealth from the Comstock Lode had far-reaching effects. It financed the Union's efforts during the Civil War, contributed to the establishment of the U.S. Mint in San Francisco, and spurred the development of the Central Pacific Railroad. The technological advancements in mining, such as the square-set timbering method and the Washoe process for extracting silver from ore, were pioneered here and revolutionized the industry.

Virginia City, at the heart of the Comstock Lode, became one of the wealthiest cities in America during its peak. The town boasted grand buildings, theaters, and luxurious hotels. The immense wealth also attracted notable figures, including Mark Twain, who worked as a reporter for the Territorial Enterprise newspaper in Virginia City.

Despite its decline in the late 19th century, the legacy of the Comstock Lode endures. The area is now a National Historic Landmark, and Virginia City preserves its rich history with museums, restored buildings, and annual events that celebrate its mining heritage.

The Comstock Lode remains a symbol of Nevada's storied past, highlighting the state's significant contributions to mining, technology, and American history.

40. Desert Research Institute: Located in Reno, the institute is a world leader in environmental and climate science research, particularly in desert environments.

41. First Neon Sign: The first neon sign in the U.S. was erected in Las Vegas in 1929, revolutionizing advertising.

42. Digital Billboards: Las Vegas pioneered the use of digital billboards, transforming the advertising landscape on the Strip.

43. Gaming Technology:

Nevada, particularly Las Vegas, is synonymous with the gambling industry, and its gaming technology has significantly evolved over the decades, making it a global leader in the field. The state's journey in gaming technology began in earnest in the 1930s when gambling was legalized, setting the stage for Nevada to become a hub of innovation and entertainment.

One of the early technological advancements was the development of the first electromechanical slot machine, the Money Honey, by Bally Manufacturing in 1963. This machine featured a bottomless hopper and automatic payouts, revolutionizing the slot machine industry. The advent of microprocessors in the 1970s further transformed slot machines, allowing for more complex game designs and random number generators, which ensured fair play and randomness.

Nevada also led the way in the development of casino management systems (CMS) and player tracking technologies. These systems allowed casinos to monitor gameplay, track player behavior, and offer personalized incentives, enhancing customer loyalty and operational efficiency. The introduction of cashless gaming and ticket-in, ticket-out (TITO) systems in the late 1990s improved convenience for players and security for casinos.

In recent years, Nevada has embraced online and mobile gaming, adapting to the digital age. The state was one of the first to legalize online poker, and its regulatory framework has become a model for other jurisdictions. The integration of advanced data analytics and artificial intelligence in gaming technology continues to enhance player experiences and optimize casino operations.

Virtual reality (VR) and augmented reality (AR) are also making inroads into the gaming world, offering immersive experiences that blend physical and digital realms. As gaming technology advances, Nevada remains at the forefront, continually shaping the future of the global gambling industry.

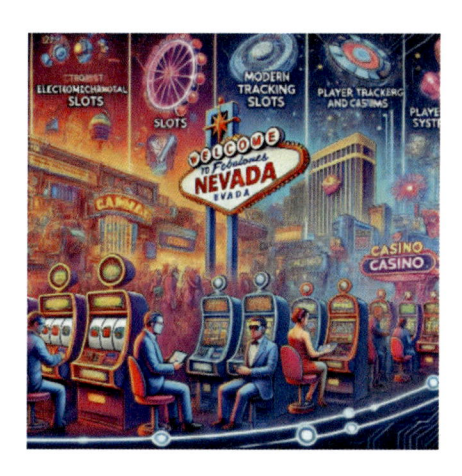

44. Nickname: Known as the "Silver State" due to its significant silver mining history.

45. The Hoover Dam: The Hoover Dam, an engineering marvel, is located on the border between Nevada and Arizona (see Volume 1/ Arizona).

46. Driest State: Nevada is the driest state in the U.S., with an average annual rainfall of only about 7 inches.

47. The Las Vegas Monorail

The Las Vegas Monorail, a state-of-the-art transportation system, offers a sleek and efficient way to navigate the bustling Las Vegas Strip. Officially opened in 2004, the monorail spans 3.9 miles, connecting major hotels and attractions from the MGM Grand to the Sahara Las Vegas.

The concept of a monorail in Las Vegas dates back to the 1990s, driven by the need to alleviate traffic congestion and provide a convenient mode of transport for the millions of tourists who visit the city annually. The current system was built on the foundations of an earlier monorail that connected the MGM Grand to Bally's, which opened in 1995. The success of this initial line led to the expansion and development of the full monorail system.

The Las Vegas Monorail is fully automated and operates on electricity, making it an environmentally friendly alternative to traditional transportation methods. Its sleek trains, running every few minutes, can reach speeds of up to 50 miles per hour, ensuring quick and efficient travel along the Strip.

The monorail's stations are strategically located near key attractions and entertainment venues, providing easy access to casinos, convention centers, and shopping areas. This convenience makes it a popular choice for both tourists and locals. Additionally, the system is designed to handle large volumes of passengers, especially during major events and conventions.

In recent years, there have been discussions about extending the monorail to connect with McCarran International Airport and other parts of the city, further enhancing its utility. Despite facing financial challenges and competition from other transportation options like ride-sharing services, the Las Vegas Monorail remains a vital part of the city's infrastructure.

The monorail not only represents a technological achievement but also underscores Las Vegas's commitment to innovation and sustainability in urban transportation.

48. Capital City: The state capital is Carson City.

49. Mountain Ranges: Nevada has more mountain ranges than any other state in the U.S.

50. Geographical Location: Nevada is located in the western region of the United States. It is bordered by several states: to the west, it shares a long border with California; to the north, it is bordered by Oregon and Idaho; to the east, it meets Utah; and to the south, it is bordered by Arizona. The state's capital is Carson City, situated near the western border, and its largest city is Las Vegas, located in the southern part of the state.

Nevada's geographical features are diverse, including vast desert landscapes, mountain ranges, and large valleys. The state is predominantly arid and semi-arid, characterized by the Great Basin Desert in the north and the Mojave Desert in the south. Prominent mountain ranges include the Sierra Nevada in the west, which forms a natural border with California, and the Ruby Mountains in the northeastern part of the state.

Lake Tahoe, a large freshwater lake, is located along the western border, shared with California. The Colorado River forms part of Nevada's southeastern border with Arizona and is home to the Hoover Dam, a significant landmark and source of hydroelectric power.

The state's central and northern regions are known for their rugged terrain and numerous mountain ranges, while the southern region, where Las Vegas is situated, is characterized by its desert climate and proximity to the Mojave Desert. The combination of its deserts, mountains, and valleys makes Nevada a state of varied and striking natural beauty.

04

NEW HAMPSHIRE

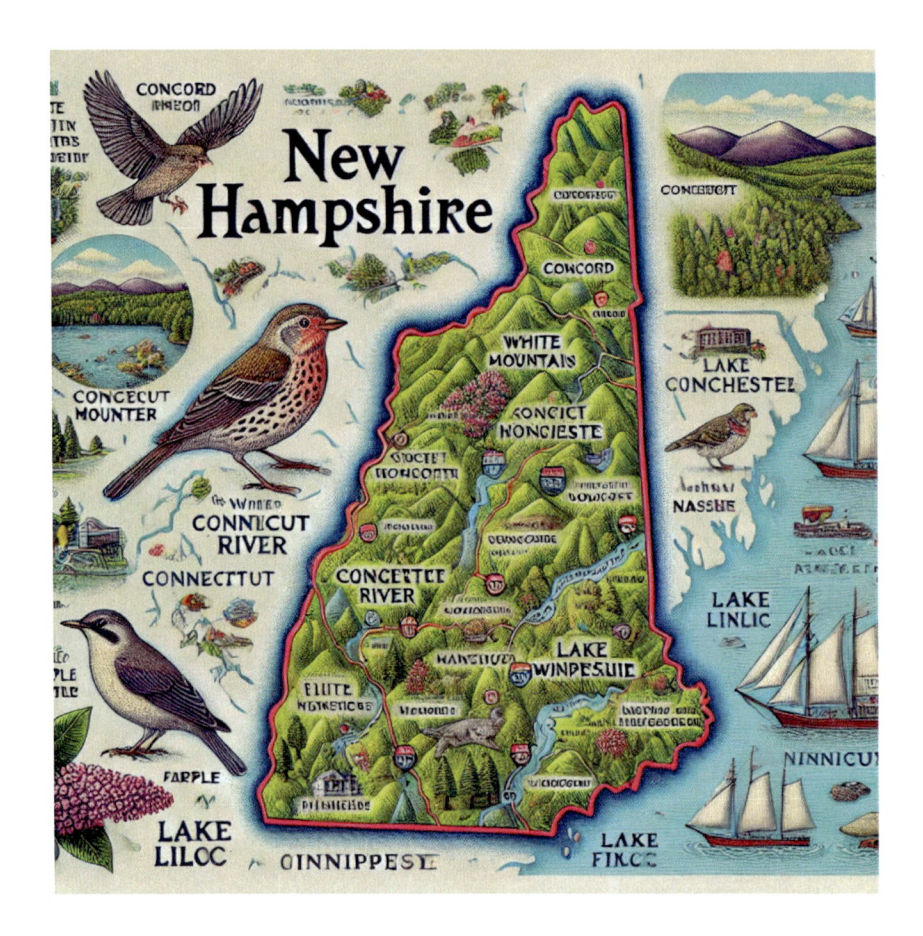

1. Battle of Bunker Hill

The Battle of Bunker Hill, fought on June 17, 1775, was a pivotal early conflict in the American Revolutionary War. Despite its name, most of the battle occurred on Breed's Hill, just outside Boston. The colonial forces, primarily from New England, including a significant number of New Hampshire soldiers, hastily fortified the area to challenge the British control of Boston. Under the command of Colonel William Prescott, the colonial militia constructed earthworks overnight.

As dawn broke, British General Thomas Gage ordered an assault to dislodge the rebels. The British troops, commanded by Major

General William Howe, launched three major frontal assaults. The first two were met with devastating fire from the entrenched American positions. The Americans famously conserved their limited ammunition, waiting to fire until they could see "the whites of their eyes," ensuring every shot counted.

Despite their valiant defense, the colonial forces eventually ran out of ammunition. In the third assault, the British troops overran the American positions, forcing a retreat. The British won the hill but suffered heavy casualties—over 1,000 soldiers were killed or wounded, compared to the Americans' 450.

The Battle of Bunker Hill was significant for several reasons. It demonstrated the Americans' willingness and ability to stand up to the British Army, boosting the morale of the colonial forces. It also showed that the British could not easily crush the rebellion, setting the stage for a prolonged and hard-fought war. For New Hampshire, the battle was a source of immense pride, as its soldiers played a critical role in the fierce defense.

2. First State Constitution: New Hampshire adopted the first written state constitution in the United States on January 5, 1776.

3. Declaration of Independence: It was the ninth state to ratify the U.S. Constitution on June 21, 1788.

4. Franklin Pierce: The 14th President of the United States, Franklin Pierce, was born in Hillsborough, New Hampshire, in 1804.

5. Old Man of the Mountain Collapse

The Old Man of the Mountain, a granite rock formation in the White Mountains of New Hampshire, was a beloved state symbol. Located in Franconia Notch, the formation resembled a craggy human profile when viewed from the north. It was naturally formed over thousands of years by the forces of erosion and weathering, standing 1,200 feet above Profile Lake.

First recorded in 1805, the Old Man of the Mountain quickly became an iconic symbol of New Hampshire's rugged beauty and resilience. The formation was featured on state signs, license plates, and the New Hampshire state quarter, becoming a source of pride for residents and a popular tourist attraction.

On May 3, 2003, the Old Man of the Mountain collapsed. Despite efforts over the years to stabilize the formation with cables and epoxy, the harsh freeze-thaw cycles of New Hampshire's climate took their toll. The collapse was a profound loss for the state. Many residents felt as though they had lost a friend, and there was an outpouring of grief and nostalgia.

In the aftermath, the state commemorated the Old Man with a memorial site at Franconia Notch. The site features a viewing area where visitors can stand and use "profilers," which are steel rods lined up to recreate the profile's appearance against the mountain background. The Old Man of the Mountain remains, and will continue to remain, an enduring symbol in New Hampshire.

6. Hannah Duston: She was the first woman in America to be honored with a statue for her actions during an Abenaki raid in 1697.

7. Black Bear Population: New Hampshire has a robust black bear population, especially in the White Mountains.

8. Monadnock Mountain: Known as one of the most climbed mountains in the world.

9. Marine Biology: The coastal town of Rye is home to the Seacoast Science Center, focusing on marine research.

10. Alan Shepard: The First American in Space

Alan Shepard, born on November 18, 1923, in Derry, New Hampshire, was a pioneer of space exploration and a national hero. Shepard's journey to becoming the first American in space began with a strong background in aviation. He graduated from the U.S. Naval Academy in 1944 and went on to become a skilled Navy test pilot. His expertise and calm demeanor under pressure caught the attention of NASA, and in 1959, he was selected as one of the original seven Mercury astronauts.

On May 5, 1961, Shepard made history aboard the Freedom 7 spacecraft. His mission, designated Mercury-Redstone 3, was a suborbital flight that lasted just 15 minutes but had a profound impact on the U.S. space program. Shepard's spacecraft reached an altitude of 116 miles and a speed of 5,134 miles per hour before safely splashing down in the Atlantic Ocean. His successful mission restored American confidence and marked a significant milestone in the space race against the Soviet Union, who had launched Yuri Gagarin into space just weeks earlier.

Shepard's achievement laid the groundwork for future manned spaceflights, including the Apollo missions. After overcoming an inner ear disorder that temporarily grounded him, Shepard commanded

Apollo 14 in 1971, becoming the fifth person to walk on the moon. His famous act of hitting two golf balls on the lunar surface captured the world's imagination and highlighted his adventurous spirit.

Alan Shepard's legacy endures in New Hampshire and across the nation. His contributions to space exploration are commemorated at the McAuliffe-Shepard Discovery Center in Concord, New Hampshire, inspiring future generations to reach for the stars.

11. Granite State: The nickname comes from its extensive granite formations and quarries.

12. New England Cottontail: Efforts are ongoing to protect this native rabbit species found in New Hampshire.

13. Forest Coverage: Approximately 84% of the state is covered by forests.

14. The First Women's Strike: Dover, 1828

The first women's strike in American history took place in Dover, New Hampshire, in December 1828. This significant event occurred at the Cocheco Manufacturing Company, a large textile mill where hundreds of young women, known as "mill girls," worked under harsh conditions. These mill girls, often in their teens and early twenties, toiled for long hours with minimal pay and little regard for their health or safety.

The catalyst for the strike was the company's decision to extend the workday from 12 to 13.5 hours while simultaneously reducing wages. This change would have significantly increased the already demanding workload without fair compensation. In response, approximately 400 women walked out of the mill in protest, an unprecedented act of defiance for that time.

The striking women organized themselves and drafted a petition demanding the restoration of their previous work hours and wages. They also appealed to the public for support, highlighting the unjust treatment they faced. Their courage and determination drew attention to the plight of industrial workers, particularly women, and sparked discussions about labor rights and fair treatment.

Though the strike was ultimately unsuccessful—the company refused to meet their demands, and many of the women were forced to return to work under the new conditions—it set a powerful precedent. The strike demonstrated the potential for organized labor to challenge oppressive practices and paved the way for future labor movements.

The Dover women's strike of 1828 is remembered as a landmark moment in labor history. It showcased the strength and resilience of women workers and highlighted the importance of solidarity and collective action in the fight for workers' rights.

15. Art Colony: The MacDowell Colony in Peterborough is a famous artists' residency program.

16. State Song: "Old New Hampshire" is the official state song, reflecting its history and natural beauty.

17. Winter Sports: The state is a popular destination for skiing and snowboarding, with many resorts in the White Mountains.

18. Poetry and Literature: Robert Frost, one of America's most famous poets, lived and wrote in New Hampshire.

19. The Highest Wind Speed Ever Recorded by Man:

On April 12, 1934, Mount Washington, New Hampshire, became famous for recording the highest wind speed ever observed by man. The Mount Washington Observatory, located at the summit, measured a wind gust of 231 miles per hour. This record-breaking event placed Mount Washington, already known for its extreme and unpredictable weather, in the meteorological history books.

Mount Washington, the highest peak in the Northeastern United States at 6,288 feet, is notorious for its severe weather conditions. The combination of its unique location, elevation, and geography results in a convergence of weather patterns that can lead to extraordinarily high wind speeds, rapid temperature changes, and intense storms.

The Mount Washington Observatory staff, a dedicated team of meteorologists and researchers, had long been aware of the mountain's fierce winds. On that fateful April day, they were conducting routine weather observations when the wind speeds began to climb. Using an anemometer, a device for measuring wind speed, they meticulously recorded the escalating gusts. The wind eventually peaked at an astonishing 231 miles per hour, a record that would stand for decades.

This remarkable measurement provided valuable data for understanding atmospheric dynamics and wind behavior. It highlighted the need for robust structures and safety protocols in extreme weather conditions. The record also cemented Mount Washington's reputation as "Home of the World's Worst Weather," attracting meteorologists, researchers, and adventure seekers from around the globe.

Today, visitors to Mount Washington can learn about this historic event at the Mount Washington Observatory and Weather Discovery Center. The legacy of the 1934 wind speed record continues to underscore the importance of weather observation and research in predicting and understanding the Earth's most extreme conditions.

20. No Helmet Law: New Hampshire is the only state in the U.S. that does not require adults to wear motorcycle helmets.

21. Independent Streak: It is known as the "Live Free or Die" state, a motto reflecting its residents' strong independent spirit.

22. Ice Harvesting: In the 19th century, New Hampshire was a major ice exporter, cutting large blocks from lakes and shipping them worldwide.

23. Purple Lilac: The state flower was chosen by the state legislature in 1919 to represent the hardy character of New Hampshire's people.

24. Mount Washington Cog Railway:

The Mount Washington Cog Railway, built in 1869, is a marvel of engineering and a testament to human ingenuity. As the world's first mountain-climbing cog railway, it provides a unique and thrilling journey to the summit of Mount Washington, the highest peak in the Northeastern United States.

The idea for the railway was conceived by Sylvester Marsh, an inventor from Campton, New Hampshire. After nearly perishing in a storm while hiking Mount Washington, Marsh was inspired to create a safer and more accessible way to reach the summit.

His vision was initially met with skepticism, with critics derisively referring to it as "Marsh's Folly." Undeterred, Marsh patented his cog railway design and secured funding to begin construction.

The construction of the railway was an enormous undertaking, involving innovative engineering solutions to navigate the steep and rugged terrain. The cog system, which uses a toothed rail and cogwheel to provide traction, allowed trains to ascend grades as steep as 37.41%. This engineering breakthrough made it possible for trains to safely climb and descend the mountain.

On July 3, 1869, the first passenger train successfully reached the summit, marking a new era in mountain travel. The railway quickly became a popular attraction, drawing visitors from all over the world to experience the breathtaking views and the thrill of the ascent. The journey offers panoramic vistas of the surrounding White Mountains, forests, and valleys, making it a memorable experience for all who ride it.

Today, the Mount Washington Cog Railway remains a beloved tourist destination and an enduring symbol of New Hampshire's pioneering spirit. It continues to operate, with both historic steam locomotives and modern biodiesel engines, providing an unforgettable journey through history and nature.

25. Oldest State House: The New Hampshire State House in Concord is the oldest state capitol where the legislature still meets in its original chambers.

26. No Income or Sales Tax in New Hampshire:

New Hampshire stands out as one of the few states in the United States that does not levy a state income tax or a general sales tax. This unique fiscal policy has earned New Hampshire the nickname "The Live Free or Die" state, reflecting its commitment to personal freedom and minimal government intervention.

The absence of these taxes is rooted in New Hampshire's history and culture. The state's residents have long valued self-reliance and limited government. This philosophy has translated into a tax structure that relies on other forms of revenue, such as property taxes, business taxes, and various fees. This approach aims to reduce the tax burden on individuals and promote economic freedom.

The lack of income and sales taxes has several implications for both residents and visitors. For residents, it means that their earnings are not subject to state income tax, allowing them to retain more of their income. This policy is particularly beneficial for retirees and high earners, who might otherwise face substantial state income taxes. For visitors, shopping in New Hampshire is attractive because goods are not subject to sales tax, making it a popular destination for people from neighboring states looking to save money on large purchases.

However, this tax structure also means that New Hampshire relies heavily on property taxes to fund public services, such as education, infrastructure, and public safety. As a result, property taxes in the state are among the highest in the nation. This reliance can create challenges, particularly for homeowners on fixed incomes and renters, as the costs are often passed down through higher rents.

Despite these challenges, New Hampshire's tax policy remains a point of pride for many residents, embodying the state's values of independence and limited government. The approach continues to attract individuals and businesses seeking a tax-friendly environment.

27. Saint-Gaudens National Historical Park: The home and studio of Augustus Saint-Gaudens, a renowned American sculptor.

28. Kancamagus Highway: A scenic byway through the White Mountains, renowned for its fall foliage.

29. The Flume Gorge: A natural gorge extending 800 feet at the base of Mount Liberty, a popular tourist destination.

30. Isles of Shoals:

The Isles of Shoals, a group of small islands located approximately six miles off the coast of New Hampshire and Maine, are steeped in history, mystery, and natural beauty. Comprising nine islands, the Shoals are divided between the two states, with four islands in New Hampshire and five in Maine. These islands have been a hub of activity for centuries, from Native American settlements to bustling fishing communities and, more recently, serene retreats.

Historically, the Isles of Shoals were first settled by Europeans in the early 17th century. The islands quickly became an important center for the fishing industry due to the rich fishing grounds surrounding them. Fishermen from England and Europe established seasonal camps to harvest cod and other fish, which were then dried and shipped back to Europe. The islands thrived as a commercial fishing outpost until the industry declined in the 19th century.

In the mid-1800s, the islands transitioned from a bustling fishing center to a popular summer resort destination. Poet Celia Thaxter, who lived on Appledore Island, brought literary and artistic figures to the Isles, creating a vibrant cultural scene. Her family's hotel, the Appledore House, became a gathering place for artists, writers, and musicians, contributing to the islands' allure.

Today, the Isles of Shoals are known for their stunning natural landscapes, historical significance, and tranquil atmosphere. Star Island, one of the largest islands, hosts a seasonal conference center and retreat operated by the Unitarian Universalist Association and the United Church of Christ. Visitors can explore historic buildings, hike scenic trails, and enjoy the pristine coastline.

The Isles of Shoals are also a site of scientific interest, with ongoing research in marine biology and ecology. The Shoals Marine Laboratory, a joint venture between Cornell University and the University of New Hampshire, conducts research and educational programs on Appledore Island.

The islands continue to captivate visitors with their blend of natural beauty, rich history, and peaceful retreat from the mainland's hustle and bustle.

31. Castle in the Clouds: A historic mansion and estate in Moultonborough with stunning views of Lake Winnipesaukee.

32. Concord: The state capital and home to the New Hampshire State House.

33. Lake Winnipesaukee: The largest lake in the state, popular for boating and fishing.

34. The Cilley Family:

The Cilley family has played a notable role in New Hampshire's history, contributing significantly to the state's political and military legacy. The family's influence spans several generations, with members distinguishing themselves in various fields, from the Revolutionary War to state politics.

One of the most prominent members of the Cilley family was General Joseph Cilley, born in 1734 in Nottingham, New Hampshire. He was a dedicated patriot who played a crucial role during the American Revolutionary War. As a colonel in the Continental Army, Cilley participated in key battles, including the Battle of Saratoga, which was a turning point in the war. His leadership and bravery earned him a promotion to brigadier general in the New Hampshire Militia after the war.

Joseph Cilley's commitment to public service extended beyond the battlefield. After the war, he served in the New Hampshire State Senate and as a state treasurer. His legacy of public service was carried on by his descendants, who continued to impact New Hampshire's political landscape.

Another notable Cilley was his grandson, Jonathan Cilley, who was born in 1802 in Nottingham. Jonathan pursued a career in law and politics, eventually serving as a U.S. Congressman from Maine. His promising career was tragically cut short in 1838 when he was killed in a duel with Congressman William Graves of Kentucky, an event that shocked the nation and highlighted the era's volatile political climate.

The Cilley family's contributions to New Hampshire are commemorated in various ways, including historical markers and preserved family homesteads. Their story is a testament to the enduring impact of one family's dedication to their state and country.

35. Horace Greeley: Founder of the New-York Tribune and famous for saying, "Go West, young man," born in Amherst.

36. New Hampshire Highland Games: Celebrates Scottish culture with traditional games, music, and dancing, held annually in Lincoln.

37. First Primary: New Hampshire holds the first primary in the U.S. presidential election cycle, giving it significant political influence.

38. Sarah Josepha Hale: Author of "Mary Had a Little Lamb" and advocate for making Thanksgiving a national holiday, born in Newport.

39. Webster-Ashburton Treaty:

The Webster-Ashburton Treaty of 1842 was a significant diplomatic agreement between the United States and Great Britain, resolving long-standing border disputes between the U.S. and British North America (now Canada). The treaty's negotiation was led by Daniel Webster, a statesman from New Hampshire, and Alexander Baring, the 1st Baron Ashburton, representing Great Britain.

The primary issue at hand was the precise delineation of the border between Maine and the British colony of New Brunswick. Tensions had escalated over competing claims, leading to the Aroostook War, a bloodless conflict between American and British-Canadian lumberjacks. Both nations sought a peaceful resolution to avoid further confrontation.

Daniel Webster, known for his eloquence and diplomatic skills, played a crucial role in the negotiations. He aimed to reach a fair agreement that would satisfy both American and British interests. The resulting treaty established a clear and mutually acceptable border, with both sides making concessions. The U.S. gained over half of the disputed territory, while Britain secured a critical trade route between Halifax and Quebec.

The Webster-Ashburton Treaty also addressed other issues beyond the Maine-New Brunswick border. It resolved the boundary between Lake Superior and the Lake of the Woods, clarified the use of shared waterways, and included provisions for cooperation in suppressing the international slave trade.

The successful negotiation of the Webster-Ashburton Treaty had lasting impacts. It strengthened U.S.-British relations, promoted stability in the border regions, and demonstrated the effectiveness of diplomacy in resolving international disputes. For Daniel Webster, it was a significant achievement in his illustrious career, showcasing his ability to navigate complex geopolitical challenges.

The treaty remains an important chapter in the history of U.S. diplomacy, highlighting the importance of skilled negotiation and compromise in maintaining peace and fostering international cooperation.

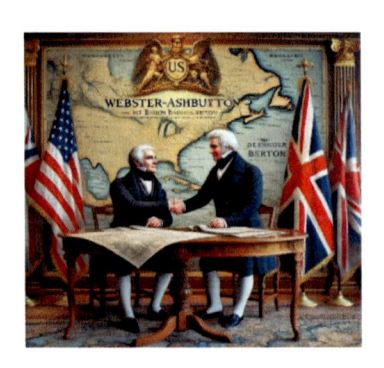

40. Laconia Motorcycle Week: One of the oldest and largest motorcycle rallies in the country, held every June.

41. Largest Arcade: Funspot in Laconia is recognized by the Guinness Book of World Records as the world's largest arcade.

42. DEKA Research & Development: Founded by Dean Kamen, known for innovations like the Segway.

43. Dartmouth College:

Dartmouth College, located in Hanover, New Hampshire, is one of the United States' prestigious Ivy League institutions. Founded in 1769 by Reverend Eleazar Wheelock, Dartmouth was established to educate Native Americans and European settlers. Its founding was rooted in Wheelock's earlier efforts to educate Native American youth through Moor's Charity School in Connecticut.

Dartmouth's early years were challenging, with limited resources and harsh New England winters. However, the college persevered and grew, attracting students and faculty committed to higher learning and societal contribution. The college's mission evolved to include a broader student body, while still honoring its original commitment to Native American education.

The Dartmouth campus is renowned for its picturesque New England setting, featuring historic buildings and expansive green spaces. Key landmarks include Baker-Berry Library, the Hopkins Center for the Arts, and the Dartmouth Green, a central gathering place for students. The college's Hood Museum of Art boasts an impressive collection, enriching the cultural and intellectual life on campus.

Dartmouth has a strong emphasis on undergraduate education, offering a liberal arts curriculum that encourages interdisciplinary study. The college also offers renowned graduate programs through its Tuck School of Business, Thayer School of Engineering, and Geisel School of Medicine.

Notable alumni include Daniel Webster, a prominent 19th-century statesman; Robert Frost, the celebrated poet; and Dr. Seuss (Theodor Geisel), the beloved children's author. Dartmouth's influence extends beyond its alumni, as the college has been a hub for intellectual and cultural exchange.

The college is also known for its traditions, such as the annual Winter Carnival, a student-organized event featuring ice sculptures, snow sports, and social activities. Dartmouth Outing Club, one of the oldest and largest collegiate outing clubs in the country, promotes outdoor activities like hiking, skiing, and canoeing, reflecting the college's connection to its natural surroundings.

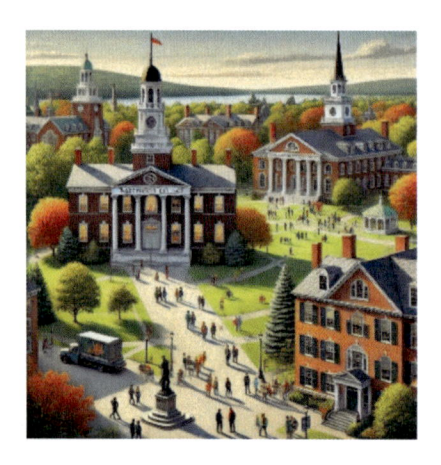

44. Merrimack River: Flows through several major cities, including Concord and Manchester.

45. Velcro USA: The American headquarters of the Velcro company is in Manchester.

46. Portsmouth Naval Shipyard: Established in 1800, it is one of the oldest continuously operating shipyards in the U.S.

47. John Stark:

John Stark, born on August 28, 1728, in Londonderry, New Hampshire, is a celebrated figure in American history, known for his crucial role in the American Revolutionary War. Stark's military career and contributions to the fight for American independence have earned him the title "The Hero of Bennington."

Stark's early life was marked by rugged frontier experiences, including his capture by Native Americans during a hunting expedition and his subsequent adoption into the tribe. These experiences honed his survival skills and deepened his understanding of Native American culture and warfare. After his release, Stark joined the New Hampshire Militia, where he quickly rose through the ranks due to his leadership abilities and bravery.

During the Revolutionary War, Stark became a prominent leader. He played a significant role in the Battle of Bunker Hill, leading New Hampshire troops with distinction. However, it was his leadership at the Battle of Bennington in 1777 that solidified his legacy. Stark's forces, comprising militia from New Hampshire, Vermont, and Massachusetts, achieved a decisive victory against British and Hessian troops. This victory was pivotal, as it contributed to the defeat of British General John Burgoyne at Saratoga, a turning point in the war.

Stark's tactical acumen and inspirational leadership were instrumental in boosting the morale of American forces. His famous rallying cry, "Live Free or Die," has become synonymous with New Hampshire's spirit of independence and resilience. After the war, Stark returned to his farm in Derryfield (now Manchester), where he lived out his life in relative obscurity but remained a revered figure.

John Stark's contributions to American independence are commemorated through various monuments, historical markers, and the annual "Stark Day" celebrations in New Hampshire. His legacy endures as a symbol of courage, leadership, and the enduring fight for freedom.

48. Craftsmanship: New Hampshire is known for its fine furniture and crafts, especially in the town of Canterbury.

49. Fort William and Mary: Captured by patriots in 1774, it's a key Revolutionary War site.

50. Geographical Location: New Hampshire is located in the New England region of the northeastern United States. It is bordered by the state of Maine to the east, the Atlantic Ocean to the southeast, Massachusetts to the south, Vermont to the west, and the Canadian province of Quebec to the north.

Geographically, New Hampshire is known for its diverse landscapes, which include the White Mountains in the northern part of the state, with Mount Washington being the highest peak in the northeastern U.S. The state's central region features the Lakes Region, highlighted by Lake Winnipesaukee, the largest lake in New Hampshire. To the south, the Merrimack River Valley is home to the state's most populous cities, including Manchester and Nashua.

New Hampshire's 18-mile coastline, the shortest of any U.S. coastal state, provides access to the Atlantic Ocean, with the city of Portsmouth serving as a historic and economic hub. The state's western border is defined by the Connecticut River, which separates it from Vermont.

New Hampshire's position in New England places it within driving distance of major metropolitan areas such as Boston, Massachusetts, to the south, and Montreal, Canada, to the north. The state is characterized by its scenic beauty, from rugged mountains and dense forests to tranquil lakes and coastal beaches, making it a popular destination for outdoor recreation and tourism.

05

NEW JERSEY

1. The Origin of the First Baseball Game:

New Jersey is home to a groundbreaking moment in American sports history—it hosted the first official game of baseball! On June 19, 1846, the New York Nine defeated the Knickerbockers 23-1 in Hoboken, New Jersey. This wasn't just a casual game; it marked the birth of organized baseball, laying down the foundation for what would become America's beloved pastime.

Imagine a sunny day, the field bustling with energy and anticipation. The players wore no gloves, and the rules were different, but the spirit of competition was just as fierce as it is today. This game wasn't merely a contest of strength and strategy; it was a showcase of a sport that would grow to symbolize American culture and values. It highlighted teamwork, fairness, and the pursuit of excellence, principles that resonate deeply in the American ethos.

The site of this historic game, the Elysian Fields in Hoboken, became a sacred ground for baseball enthusiasts. Although professional baseball would evolve with stadiums, floodlights, and modern equipment, the essence of the game—its ability to unite people, spark joy, and inspire dreams—remains unchanged.

This event isn't just a footnote in sports history; it's a testament to innovation and the enduring appeal of baseball. It reminds us that great things often have humble beginnings, and that with passion and perseverance, any field in America can be the birthplace of the next great tradition.

2. Birthplace of Famous Inventors: Albert Einstein made Princeton, New Jersey, his home after fleeing Nazi Germany in 1933.

3. Monopoly Board Game: The streets in the original Monopoly board game are named after actual streets in Atlantic City.

4. The Jersey Tomato: New Jersey is famous for its tomatoes, considered some of the best in the world

5.The Invention of the Light Bulb:

Thomas Edison, one of the greatest inventors in history, made a breakthrough that would illuminate the world—the invention of the practical electric light bulb. This monumental achievement took place in Menlo Park, New Jersey, in 1879. Edison's invention was not just about bringing light into dark rooms; it was about igniting the potential for human advancement. The light bulb symbolized the dawn of a new era, transforming industries, lifestyles, and societies.

Before Edison's invention, people relied on gas lamps and candles, which were not only inefficient but also hazardous. The electric light bulb led to longer working hours, safer streets at night, and the eventual development of countless electrical appliances that make our lives easier today.

Edison's work in New Jersey wasn't a solo effort; it involved teamwork and persistence. His lab, often called the "Invention Factory," was a hub of creativity and innovation. Here, Edison and his team experimented with thousands of materials to find the perfect filament for the light bulb, ultimately discovering that carbonized bamboo worked best.

This invention is a powerful reminder of the impact one person's curiosity and determination can have on the world. It shows that with enough dedication, anyone can turn a bright idea into a reality that lights up the world.

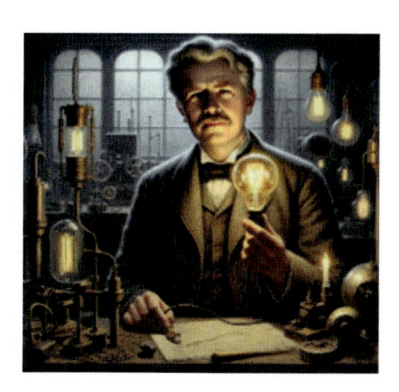

6. Largest Collection of Cherry Blossoms: Newark's Branch Brook Park has over 5,000 cherry blossom trees, more than Washington D.C.

7. First College Football Game: Rutgers University hosted the first ever college football game against Princeton in 1869.

8. Oldest Seashore Resort: Cape May is considered the country's oldest seashore resort, dating back to the mid-18th century.

9. High Point State Park: The highest point in New Jersey is located here, offering stunning views of the surrounding area.

10. The Iconic Jersey Shore:

New Jersey's coastline, affectionately known as the Jersey Shore, spans nearly 130 miles and is a beloved summer destination for both locals and visitors from around the world. This iconic shoreline is famed for its beautiful beaches, bustling boardwalks, historic lighthouses, and vibrant coastal communities. Each beach town along the shore has its own unique charm, from the family-friendly Ocean City to the lively nightlife of Seaside Heights.

Imagine walking along the boardwalk, the smell of saltwater in the air, the sound of waves crashing, and the sight of children building sandcastles while families and friends gather to create lasting memories. The Jersey Shore is more than just a series of beaches; it's a summer tradition, a place where every visit has the potential to offer new adventures. From the historic Victorian homes of Cape May to the amusement parks that light up the night sky, the shore encapsulates the spirit of New Jersey's coastal culture.

This coastline also plays a crucial role in the state's economy, drawing millions of tourists each year and supporting local businesses. Beyond its economic impact, the shore is a testament to New Jersey's resilience, particularly in the way communities came together to rebuild after Superstorm Sandy in 2012.

The Jersey Shore exemplifies the joy of summertime leisure, the beauty of the Atlantic coast, and the strength of community. It's a place where history, nature, and culture intermingle, offering endless opportunities for exploration and fun.

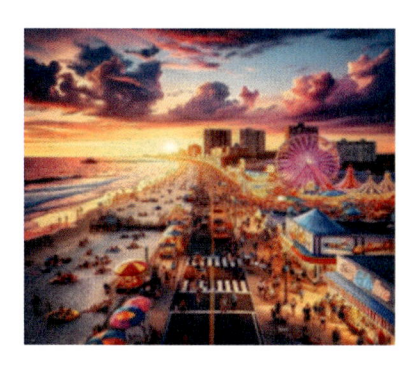

11. The Liberty Science Center: Located in Jersey City, it's one of the largest science centers in the U.S.

12. Diner Capital of the World: New Jersey has more diners than any other state.

13. The Holland Tunnel: The first mechanically ventilated underwater tunnel in the world, connecting New Jersey with New York City.

14. New Jersey's Pivotal Role in the American Revolution:

New Jersey's strategic location earned it the nickname "The Crossroads of the Revolution" during the American Revolutionary War. Sandwiched between the British stronghold in New York City and the American capital in Philadelphia, New Jersey was the stage for over 100 battles and skirmishes, more than any other state. These conflicts were not just military engagements; they were the struggles of a nascent nation fighting for its identity and freedom.

One of the most dramatic moments in New Jersey's Revolutionary history occurred on the cold, moonless night of December 25, 1776. General George Washington and his Continental Army, desperate for a victory to turn the tide of war, embarked on a daring maneuver. They crossed the ice-choked Delaware River in complete silence, surprising the Hessian forces in Trenton the following morning. This victory, followed by a decisive win at Princeton, reignited the American cause and proved pivotal in the overall course of the war.

These battles on New Jersey soil were not just military victories; they symbolized the resilience, bravery, and determination of the American spirit. Towns like Trenton, Princeton, and Morristown became etched into the fabric of American history, not just as battle sites, but as beacons of hope during the nation's darkest hours.

New Jersey's contribution to the American Revolution goes beyond the battlefield. It was a hotbed of espionage, diplomacy, and the ideological struggle for independence. The state's geography made it a corridor for troops and information, shaping the war's outcome.

The legacy of the Revolution in New Jersey is a testament to the strategic significance of geography in warfare and the enduring spirit of those who fight for their beliefs. It reminds us that freedom is often forged in the fires of conflict, and the path to independence is paved with resilience and courage.

15. First Submarine Ride: Inventor John Holland took the first submarine ride in the Passaic River in 1878.

16. Thomas Edison National Historical Park: Located in West Orange, it preserves Edison's laboratory and residence.

17. The Pine Barrens: This 1.1 million-acre preserve is the largest body of open space on the Mid-Atlantic seaboard.

18. Princeton Battlefield State Park: Site of a pivotal battle during the American Revolutionary War.

19. The Hindenburg Disaster:

One of the most dramatic events in aviation history, the Hindenburg disaster, occurred at the Naval Air Station Lakehurst in New Jersey on May 6, 1937. The German passenger airship LZ 129 Hindenburg, one of the largest aircraft ever built, caught fire and was destroyed during its attempt to dock with its mooring mast. Out of the 97 people on board, 36 were killed along with one worker on the ground. This catastrophic event marked the end of the airship era as a means of passenger transport.

The Hindenburg had been a symbol of Nazi Germany's technological advancement and national pride, completing many transatlantic journeys before the disaster. Its destruction was not only a tragic loss of life but also a significant moment in world history, signaling the vulnerability of humanity's technological achievements. The cause of the Hindenburg disaster remains a subject of debate, with theories ranging from sabotage to static electricity sparking the highly flammable hydrogen gas.

The event was one of the first disasters to receive near-instantaneous global coverage, partly due to the presence of film crews, photographers, and radio broadcaster Herbert Morrison, whose emotional eyewitness report became iconic: "Oh, the humanity!" This coverage made the Hindenburg disaster a lasting symbol of the potential dangers of early aviation and a turning point in the safety standards of passenger air travel.

20. Largest Solar Telescope: The world's largest solar telescope was at the High Point Observatory in Wantage.

21. Oldest Weekly Newspaper: The New Jersey Herald, founded in 1829, is the oldest.

22. First American Brewery: Established in Hoboken in 1642 by the Dutch settlers.

23. Blueberry Capital of the World: Hammonton holds this title, hosting an annual blueberry festival.

24. The Princeton University Legacy:

Founded in 1746, Princeton University is one of the oldest and most prestigious universities in the United States. Originally named the College of New Jersey, it was located in Elizabeth for a year and then in Newark for nine years before moving to Princeton in 1756. Princeton has a long history of academic excellence and has been the alma mater of numerous influential figures, including two U.S. Presidents, James Madison and Woodrow Wilson, who also served as the university's president before his political career.

Princeton University's campus is renowned for its beautiful Gothic architecture, sprawling greens, and historic buildings, like Nassau Hall, which once served as the temporary capital of the United States in 1783. The university has made significant contributions to various fields of study and boasts a faculty and alumni list that includes over 40 Nobel laureates.

Beyond its academic achievements, Princeton is also known for its vibrant student life, traditions, and commitment to service. One of the university's most famous traditions is the annual Princeton-Yale football game, part of the long-standing rivalry between the two Ivy League schools.

Princeton University represents the fusion of historic legacy with the pursuit of knowledge and innovation. Its contributions to education, research, and society at large underscore the vital role of higher education in shaping leaders and advancing human understanding.

25. Invention of the Motion Picture Camera: Thomas Edison also accomplished this feat in New Jersey.

26. The Origin of the Boardwalk

Atlantic City, New Jersey, is home to the world's first boardwalk, a landmark that has become synonymous with the American seaside experience. Built in 1870, the Atlantic City Boardwalk was originally constructed to keep sand out of hotel lobbies and railroad cars. This innovative solution quickly evolved into much more than a mere functional structure; it became a cultural phenomenon, setting the standard for beachside leisure and entertainment.

Spanning several miles along the coast, the boardwalk introduced the concept of a dedicated promenade for visitors to enjoy the ocean views without the inconvenience of sand in their shoes. It was lined with shops, restaurants, and attractions, offering everything from high-end boutiques to carnival-style amusements. Over the years, it has seen grand casinos, historic hotels, and the famous Steel Pier, which hosted entertainment legends and introduced the world to the spectacle of the Diving Horse.

The Atlantic City Boardwalk's impact on popular culture is immeasurable, providing the backdrop for countless movies, songs, and memories. It symbolizes the joy of summer, the allure of the shore, and the American spirit of innovation and enjoyment. Today, despite challenges and changes, it remains a beloved destination, drawing millions of visitors each year who come to stroll along its historic planks, reliving the magic that has enchanted generations.

27. Sandy Hook Lighthouse: The oldest operating lighthouse in the United States, located in Highlands, New Jersey.

28. First National Historic Park: Morristown National Historical Park was designated as the first.

29. Garden State Parkway: One of the busiest toll highways in the United States.

30. The Jersey Devil Legend:

New Jersey is also home to one of the most intriguing legends in American folklore - the Jersey Devil. According to legend, the Jersey Devil was born in the 18th century to Mother Leeds, her 13th child, in the Pine Barrens, a vast stretch of wilderness that still covers a significant part of southern New Jersey. The tale goes that upon its birth, the child transformed into a creature with hooves, a goat's head, bat wings, and a forked tail, then flew up the chimney and into the dark forests of the Pine Barrens, where it has supposedly lived ever since.

This story has captivated the imaginations of New Jersey residents and beyond for centuries, with numerous "sightings" of the creature reported over the years. Schools closed due to Jersey Devil hysteria in 1909, and the legend has inspired books, films, and even a professional hockey team name—the New Jersey Devils.

But beyond the spine-tingling tales, the legend of the Jersey Devil speaks to the rich folklore and the mysteries of the natural world that still remain untamed. The Pine Barrens themselves are a place of beauty and biodiversity, offering a stark contrast to the urban areas that many associate with New Jersey. The story of the Jersey Devil is a reminder of the state's diverse landscapes and its capacity to inspire stories that endure for generations.

31. Lucy the Elephant: A six-story elephant-shaped building located in Margate City, built in 1881.

32. First Miss America Pageant: Held in Atlantic City in 1921.

33. Birthplace of Frank Sinatra: The iconic American singer was born in Hoboken.

34. The Discovery of the First Dinosaur Skeleton in America:

In 1858, the first nearly complete dinosaur skeleton in America was discovered in Haddonfield, New Jersey. This groundbreaking find was of a dinosaur later named Hadrosaurus foulkii, which means "Foulke's bulky lizard." The discovery was pivotal because it was the first time scientists and the public realized that dinosaurs were real, massive creatures that once roamed the Earth, changing our understanding of the planet's history forever.

The Hadrosaurus foulkii was a duck-billed dinosaur that lived approximately 80 million years ago during the Late Cretaceous period. Its discovery sparked widespread public interest and led to the early field of American paleontology's growth. This dinosaur was significant not just for its size but for how it changed scientific thought regarding prehistoric life and led to the search for more dinosaur fossils across America and the world.

The find in New Jersey is a testament to the state's historical significance and its contribution to science. The story of the Hadrosaurus foulkii discovery inspires curiosity and wonder, encouraging young minds to explore the natural world and its ancient mysteries.

35. The New Jersey Turnpike: One of the most trafficked roadways in the United States.

36. M&M's Production: Hackettstown is home to a major Mars chocolate factory, where M&M's are produced.

37. Cape May Diamonds: Naturally polished quartz pebbles found on the beaches of Cape May.

38. Nellie Bly Amusement Park: Named after the pioneering journalist, located in Bordentown.

39. The Saltwater Taffy of Atlantic City:

Atlantic City is famous for many things, but perhaps one of the sweetest is the invention of saltwater taffy. According to legend, this confection was created in the 1880s when a storm flooded a candy store along the boardwalk, soaking all the taffy with salty ocean water. The next day, when a young girl asked for taffy, the owner jokingly offered her "salt water taffy." To his surprise, she loved it, and the name stuck.

This accident led to one of the most iconic treats of the Jersey Shore, embodying the spirit of innovation and the serendipity that often accompanies it. Saltwater taffy became a staple of Atlantic City, with visitors flocking to the boardwalk to try the chewy, sweet, and slightly salty candy that comes in a rainbow of colors and flavors.

The story of saltwater taffy is a delicious slice of New Jersey's cultural heritage, representing the whimsy and delight that the state's seaside has offered to millions of visitors over the years.

40. The USS New Jersey: The most decorated battleship in U.S. naval history, now a museum ship in Camden.

41. The Great Swamp National Wildlife Refuge: A critical wetland habitat for migratory birds.

42. Palisades Interstate Park: Offers over 30 miles of hiking trails along the Hudson River.

43. The Innovation of the Drive-In Movie Theater:

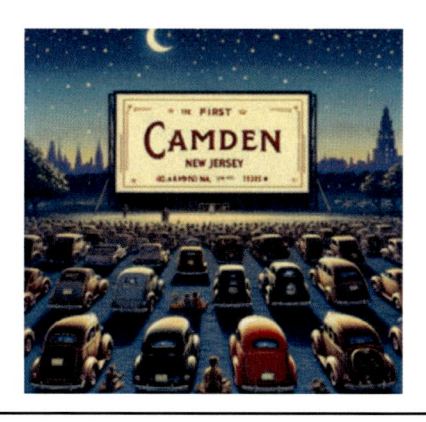

On June 6, 1933, Camden, New Jersey, became the birthplace of a uniquely American cultural phenomenon—the drive-in movie theater. Richard Hollingshead Jr., inspired by a desire to combine the comfort of automobiles with the magic of cinema, embarked on a venture that would forever alter the movie-going experience. After experimenting with various projector and sound setups in his own driveway, Hollingshead patented his invention, paving the way for the first-ever drive-in theater, dubbed "Park-In Theaters."

The inaugural screening of "Wives Beware" under the stars marked more than just an evening of entertainment; it represented a revolution in the way people watched films. Families and friends gathered in their cars, with the sprawling night sky above them, to enjoy movies in a new, communal yet intimate setting. The design of the drive-in catered to the American fondness for automobiles, allowing people to enjoy films from the privacy and comfort of their own vehicles. This innovative concept featured a gigantic 40-foot by 50-foot screen and a rudimentary yet effective sound system that transmitted the movie's audio directly to the audience in their parked cars.

The drive-in movie theater quickly captured the American imagination, leading to a boom in the mid-20th century with thousands of drive-ins sprouting across the country. Though their numbers have dwindled, the nostalgia and charm of drive-in theaters continue to captivate. New Jersey's contribution to this slice of Americana not only highlights the state's inventive spirit but also its role in shaping leisure and entertainment in the United States. The drive-in theater remains a beloved relic of American culture, offering a unique blend of communal experience and personal space within the sanctuary of one's car under the open sky.

44. Red Bank's Count Basie Theatre: Named after the famous jazz musician and Red Bank native.

45. The Stone Pony in Asbury Park: A launching pad for numerous famous music acts, including Bruce Springsteen.

46. First State to Sign the Bill of Rights: New Jersey was the first of the original 13 states to sign the Bill of Rights, cementing its place in American history as a leader in recognizing and codifying individual freedoms and legal protections.

47. The Great Falls of the Passaic River:

Nestled in the city of Paterson, New Jersey, the Great Falls of the Passaic River is one of the most spectacular natural landmarks in the United States. Standing at 77 feet high, these powerful waterfalls are a testament to the natural beauty and geological history of the region. The Great Falls are not only a stunning visual spectacle but also played a crucial role in the early industrial development of the United States.

In 1791, Alexander Hamilton, one of the founding fathers of the United States, recognized the potential of the Great Falls as a source of power for manufacturing. This vision led to the establishment of the Society for Establishing Useful Manufactures (S.U.M.), which aimed to harness the falls' power. The initiative resulted in the creation of one of the nation's first planned industrial cities,

Paterson, which earned the nickname "Silk City" for its dominant silk production industry in the 19th century.

The Great Falls symbolize the ingenuity and entrepreneurial spirit of early American industry, showcasing how natural resources can be utilized for economic development while preserving their beauty for future generations. In 2009, the falls were designated a National Historical Park, ensuring their protection and recognizing their significance in American history.

This natural wonder not only highlights New Jersey's rich industrial heritage but also its commitment to conserving natural beauty. The Great Falls of the Passaic River remain a powerful reminder of nature's force and beauty, attracting visitors from around the world to marvel at this magnificent sight.

48. Origin of the Ice Cream Cone: According to some accounts, the ice cream cone was popularized if not invented at the 1904 World's Fair by a New Jersey resident named Charles E. Menches. This sweet invention has since become a staple of American summer cuisine, enjoyed by millions across the country and around the world.

49. Birthplace of the Barcode: On June 26, 1974, the first item ever to be scanned with a UPC barcode was a 10-pack of Wrigley's Juicy Fruit gum at a supermarket in Troy Hills, New Jersey. This event marked the beginning of the use of barcode technology in retail, revolutionizing inventory management and shopping worldwide.

50. Geographical Location: New Jersey is located in the Mid-Atlantic region of the northeastern United States. It is bordered by New York to the north and northeast, the Atlantic Ocean to the east and southeast, Delaware to the southwest, and Pennsylvania to the west.

New Jersey is one of the smallest states by area but is densely populated and highly urbanized, especially in its northeastern and southwestern regions. The state's geography is diverse, featuring coastal plains, rolling hills, and pine forests. The Atlantic Ocean coastline stretches over 130 miles, from Sandy Hook in the north to Cape May in the south, featuring numerous beaches and resort towns.

Major rivers defining New Jersey's borders include the Hudson River to the northeast, the Delaware River to the west, and the Delaware Bay to the southwest. The state is divided into several distinct regions:

North Jersey: Characterized by the Highlands and the Appalachian Valley, with significant urban centers like Newark and Jersey City, part of the New York metropolitan area.

Central Jersey: Features a mix of suburban and rural areas, with cities like Trenton (the state capital) and Princeton.

South Jersey: Known for its agricultural lands, the Pine Barrens, and the bustling shore towns like Atlantic City and Cape May.

New Jersey's strategic location places it within easy reach of major metropolitan areas such as New York City to the northeast and Philadelphia to the west, contributing to its economic vitality and cultural diversity. The state's well-developed transportation infrastructure includes major highways, airports, and ports, facilitating connectivity and commerce.

06

NEW MEXICO

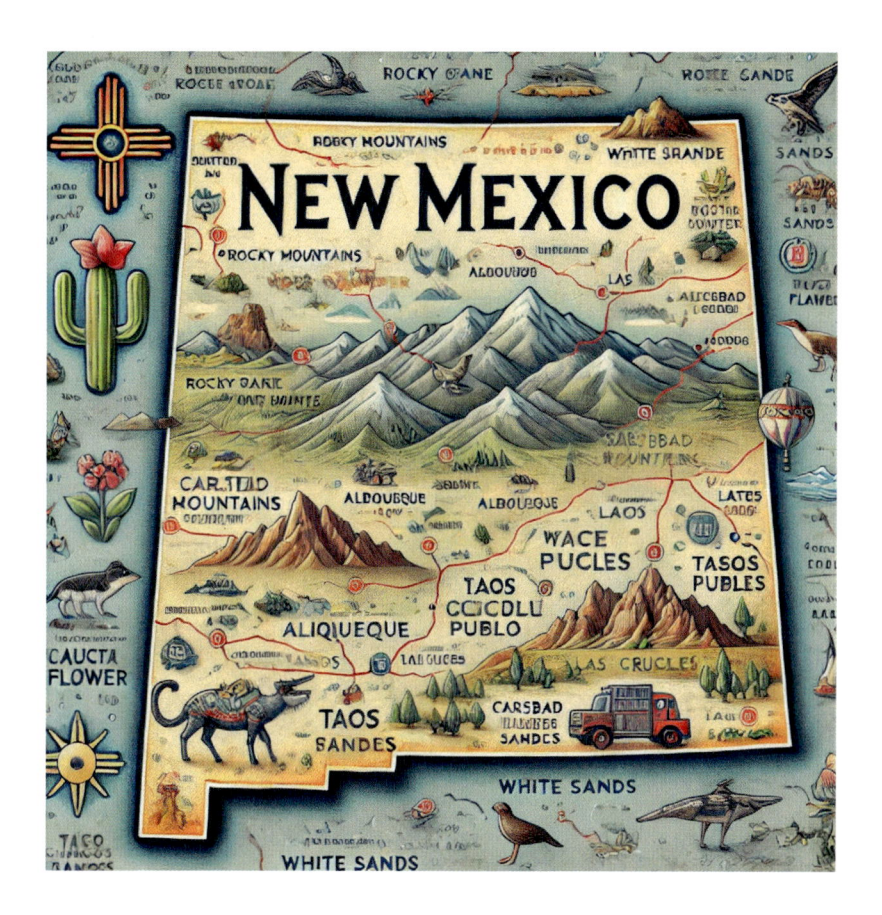

1. Trinity Test

    The Trinity Test, conducted on July 16, 1945, was the world's first detonation of a nuclear weapon. It marked a pivotal moment in history, signifying both the culmination of years of scientific research and the beginning of the atomic age. The test took place in the Jornada del Muerto desert in New Mexico, within the White Sands Proving Ground, now known as the White Sands Missile Range.

The Trinity Test was the result of the Manhattan Project, a top-secret World War II program aimed at developing nuclear weapons before Nazi Germany. Under the scientific leadership of J. Robert

Oppenheimer and the military direction of General Leslie Groves, the project brought together some of the brightest minds in physics and engineering. The primary goal was to harness the power of nuclear fission to create a weapon of unprecedented destructive capability.

In the early hours of July 16, 1945, the device, nicknamed "Gadget," was hoisted atop a 100-foot steel tower. At precisely 5:29 AM, the bomb was detonated, releasing an explosion equivalent to approximately 20 kilotons of TNT. The blast produced a blinding flash of light visible for over 200 miles and a mushroom cloud that rose to over 7 miles in height. The intense heat fused the desert sand into a green, glassy substance known as trinitite.

The success of the Trinity Test had profound implications. It confirmed that nuclear weapons were not only feasible but also immensely powerful, significantly influencing the decision to use atomic bombs on Hiroshima and Nagasaki, which ultimately led to the end of World War II. The test also marked the beginning of the nuclear arms race and ushered in an era of both scientific advancement and existential peril.

Today, the Trinity Site is a National Historic Landmark, open to the public twice a year. Visitors can view the remnants of the test, including the obelisk marking Ground Zero and pieces of trinitite, and reflect on the monumental impact of that fateful day in the New Mexico desert.

2. New Mexico Statehood: New Mexico became the 47th state of the U.S. on January 6, 1912.

3. Gadsden Purchase: In 1853, the U.S. acquired land from Mexico, including parts of modern-day New Mexico.

4. Battle of Glorieta Pass: A key Civil War battle in New Mexico, sometimes called the "Gettysburg of the West."

5. Los Alamos:

Los Alamos, New Mexico, is a town with a profound historical significance due to its central role in the development of the atomic bomb during World War II. Nestled on the Pajarito Plateau, Los Alamos was chosen as the site for the top-secret laboratory of the Manhattan Project, primarily for its remote location and existing infrastructure from a previous boys' school.

In 1942, J. Robert Oppenheimer, a brilliant physicist, was appointed scientific director of the Manhattan Project. He recommended Los Alamos as the ideal location for the laboratory where the world's first nuclear weapons would be developed. The town was swiftly transformed into a high-security military installation, attracting some of the most renowned scientists of the time, including Enrico Fermi, Richard Feynman, and Niels Bohr.

The primary goal at Los Alamos was to design and build an atomic bomb. Scientists worked under intense secrecy and pressure, conducting groundbreaking research in nuclear physics and engineering. Their efforts culminated in the successful Trinity Test on July 16, 1945 as mentioned in Fact #1 above, proving that nuclear weapons were not only feasible but also incredibly powerful.

The success of the Manhattan Project at Los Alamos led to the production of the bombs dropped on Hiroshima and Nagasaki, which played a crucial role in ending World War II. The work done at Los Alamos had far-reaching implications, ushering in the nuclear age and significantly altering global geopolitics.

After the war, Los Alamos National Laboratory (LANL) continued to be a leading center for scientific research and innovation. Today, LANL conducts research in various fields, including national security, space exploration, renewable energy, and medicine. The town of Los Alamos, once shrouded in secrecy, has grown into a vibrant community with a rich history.

Visitors to Los Alamos can explore its storied past through the Bradbury Science Museum, which offers exhibits on the Manhattan Project, nuclear science, and the lab's ongoing research. The Los Alamos Historical Museum provides further insight into the town's unique heritage, making it a compelling destination for those interested in science, history, and the profound events that shaped the modern world.

6. White Sands: The world's largest gypsum dunefield, covering 275 square miles.

7. Pueblo Revolt: In 1680, the Pueblo people successfully revolted against Spanish colonization, temporarily driving out settlers.

8. Route 66: The famous highway passes through New Mexico, including the cities of Albuquerque and Gallup.

9. Hot Springs: The town of Truth or Consequences is known for its geothermal hot springs.

10. Valley of Fires Recreation Area:

The Valley of Fires Recreation Area, located near Carrizozo, New Mexico, is a remarkable geological site featuring one of the most recent lava flows in the continental United States. The lava field, known as the Carrizozo Malpais, was formed approximately 5,000 years ago from volcanic eruptions along a 44-mile-long fissure. This vast expanse of basaltic lava covers about 125 square miles, creating a unique and rugged landscape.

The lava flow's surface is dotted with numerous features typical of volcanic terrains, including lava tubes, pressure ridges, and deep fissures. These formations create a dramatic and otherworldly environment that is fascinating to explore. The black, jagged rocks contrast strikingly with the surrounding desert vegetation, making the Valley of Fires a visual spectacle.

Despite the harsh conditions, the lava field supports a surprising diversity of plant and animal life. Hardy species such as the yucca, prickly pear cactus, and various lichens have adapted to thrive in this environment. The area is also home to a range of wildlife, including lizards, snakes, and small mammals. Birdwatchers can spot species such as hawks, owls, and various songbirds that inhabit the area.

Visitors to the Valley of Fires Recreation Area can enjoy a variety of activities. A well-maintained boardwalk trail allows for easy exploration of the lava field, offering interpretive signs that explain the geological history and natural features of the area. There are also picnic areas, campsites, and opportunities for hiking, photography, and stargazing. The clear, dark skies of the New Mexico desert provide excellent conditions for observing stars and planets.

The Valley of Fires is a testament to the dynamic geological processes that shape our planet. It offers a unique opportunity to witness the raw power of nature and the beauty that arises from such dramatic events.

11. Meteorite Crater: The state has multiple meteorite impact sites, including the Clayton Lake site.

12. Sandia Mountains: These mountains rise to over 10,000 feet and are part of the Rocky Mountains.

13. Rio Grande Rift: A geological feature that forms part of the boundary between the Pacific and North American plates. The Rio Grande river runs from Colorado through New Mexico to the Gulf of Mexico.

14. Santa Fe:

Santa Fe, the capital of New Mexico, is renowned for its rich history, vibrant culture, and stunning architecture. Established in 1610, it is the oldest state capital in the United States, with a heritage deeply influenced by Native American, Spanish, and Mexican traditions. Nestled in the foothills of the Sangre de Cristo Mountains, Santa Fe is known for its picturesque setting and unique adobe buildings.

The city's historic heart is the Plaza, a central gathering place surrounded by shops, galleries, and museums. The Palace of the

Governors, located on the north side of the Plaza, is the oldest continuously occupied public building in the United States. Originally serving as the seat of government for the Spanish colony, it now houses a museum showcasing New Mexico's history and culture.

Santa Fe is a hub for the arts, often called "The City Different." It boasts a thriving arts scene with numerous galleries, museums, and cultural institutions. The Georgia O'Keeffe Museum celebrates the life and work of the iconic artist, who drew much of her inspiration from the New Mexican landscape. Canyon Road, a historic street lined with galleries, offers a diverse array of contemporary and traditional art.

The city is also known for its vibrant festivals and events. The Santa Fe Indian Market, held every August, is the largest Native American art market in the world, attracting artists and collectors from around the globe. The Santa Fe Opera, an internationally acclaimed company, performs in an open-air theater with breathtaking views of the surrounding mountains.

Santa Fe's culinary scene is equally notable, blending Native American, Spanish, and Mexican flavors. The city is famous for its green and red chile, which features prominently in local dishes. Food enthusiasts can explore a variety of restaurants, farmers' markets, and food festivals that highlight regional cuisine.

Santa Fe's blend of history, culture, and natural beauty makes it a unique and enchanting destination. Its commitment to preserving its heritage while embracing contemporary arts and cuisine ensures that there is something for everyone to enjoy.

15. Carlsbad Caverns National Park: Known for its extensive underground limestone caves.

16. Bandera Ice Cave: A unique attraction where ice forms inside a volcanic cave.

17. Chaco Culture National Historical Park: Preserves one of the most important pre-Columbian cultural and historical areas in the U.S.

18. Gila Cliff Dwellings: Ancient dwellings built into the cliffs by the Mogollon people.

19. Billy the Kid:

Billy the Kid, born Henry McCarty and also known as William H. Bonney, is one of the most legendary outlaws of the American West. His life and exploits have become the stuff of folklore, particularly in New Mexico, where he spent much of his short but eventful life.

Born in 1859, Billy the Kid's early life was marked by hardship and instability. Orphaned at a young age, he turned to a life of petty crime to survive. By his late teens, Billy had developed a reputation as a skilled gunfighter and horse thief. His charm, boyish good looks, and notorious exploits quickly made him a folk hero and an outlaw legend.

Billy the Kid's most famous escapades occurred during the Lincoln County War, a violent feud between rival factions vying for control of commerce and land in Lincoln County, New Mexico. Billy sided with the Regulators, a group opposed to the powerful and corrupt Murphy-Dolan faction. During this conflict, he allegedly participated in several gunfights, cementing his reputation as a deadly gunslinger.

In 1880, Billy the Kid was captured by Sheriff Pat Garrett and sentenced to hang for the murder of Sheriff William Brady. However, in a daring escape from the Lincoln County Courthouse, he killed two deputies and fled, evading capture for several months. On July

14, 1881, Garrett tracked Billy to Fort Sumner, New Mexico, and shot him dead. Billy was just 21 years old.

Despite his brief life, Billy the Kid's legacy endures. He remains an iconic figure in American folklore, symbolizing the lawlessness and romance of the Wild West. His life has been immortalized in countless books, songs, and movies. Visitors to New Mexico can explore various historical sites associated with Billy the Kid, including his grave in Fort Sumner, the Lincoln Historic Site, and the Billy the Kid Museum in Fort Sumner, which offer a glimpse into the life and times of this infamous outlaw.

20. Chimayo Chile: The tiny village of Chimayo produces a unique variety of red chile pepper that is highly prized by chefs and food enthusiasts.

21. Breaking Bad: Albuquerque is the filming location for the hit TV series "Breaking Bad," with many tours and attractions related to the show.

22. New Mexico United: A professional soccer team competing in the USL Championship.

23. Valles Caldera: A large volcanic caldera that is a hotbed for geothermal activity and diverse wildlife.

24. The Very Large Array:

The Very Large Array (VLA), located on the Plains of San Agustin in central New Mexico, is one of the world's premier astronomical radio observatories. Operated by the National Radio Astronomy Observatory (NRAO), the VLA consists of 27 large radio antennas arranged in a Y-shaped configuration, each dish measuring 82 feet in diameter. Together, they function as a single, massive radio telescope.

Since its completion in 1980, the VLA has been at the forefront of astronomical research, contributing to numerous groundbreaking discoveries. It operates by detecting radio waves emitted by celestial objects, allowing astronomers to study phenomena that are invisible to optical telescopes. This capability has provided invaluable insights into the structure and evolution of the universe.

The VLA has played a crucial role in studying quasars, pulsars, black holes, and the distribution of hydrogen in galaxies. It has also been instrumental in mapping the Milky Way and observing distant galaxies and star-forming regions. One of its most famous contributions was helping to image the first direct evidence of a black hole at the center of the Milky Way galaxy.

Visitors to the VLA can embark on a self-guided walking tour of the facility. The tour includes stops at the antennas, the control center, and the visitor center, which features exhibits on radio astronomy, the history of the VLA, and its scientific achievements. Additionally, guided tours and special events are periodically offered, providing deeper insights into the workings of this remarkable observatory.

The VLA's iconic, futuristic appearance has made it a popular location for films and television, including the movie "Contact," which showcased its impressive capabilities and the human quest for understanding the cosmos.

Nestled in the remote New Mexico desert, the Very Large Array stands as a demonstration of human curiosity and ingenuity, continually expanding our knowledge of the universe.

25. Red River Memorial Day Motorcycle Rally: A large motorcycle rally attracting riders from across the country.

26. Taos Pueblo:

Taos Pueblo, located in northern New Mexico, is one of the oldest continuously inhabited communities in the United States. This ancient pueblo has been home to the Tiwa-speaking Native American people for over 1,000 years. Recognized as both a UNESCO World Heritage Site and a National Historic Landmark, Taos Pueblo is renowned for its unique adobe architecture and rich cultural heritage.

The pueblo consists of multi-storied adobe buildings made from earth, straw, and water, sun-dried into bricks. These structures are remarkably well-preserved, offering a glimpse into the traditional way of life that has been maintained for centuries. The iconic multi-story buildings, particularly the North House (Hlauuma) and the South House (Hlaukwima), are the most photographed and recognized images of Taos Pueblo.

The community of Taos Pueblo remains vibrant and active, with about 150 people living full-time within the pueblo walls. The residents continue to practice traditional customs, arts, and crafts. The pueblo is famous for its beautiful pottery, handcrafted jewelry, and intricate beadwork, which are highly sought after by collectors and visitors.

The spiritual and cultural life of the pueblo is deeply rooted in tradition. The residents practice a blend of their ancient native religion and Catholicism, a legacy of Spanish colonization. The San Geronimo Church, originally built in the 1600s and rebuilt after being destroyed in the 19th century, stands as a symbol of this cultural synthesis.

Visitors to Taos Pueblo can explore the historic buildings, engage with local artisans, and learn about the pueblo's history and traditions through guided tours. The pueblo also hosts several annual events, such as the San Geronimo Feast Day in late September, which features traditional dances, ceremonies, and a vibrant arts and crafts fair.

Taos Pueblo's enduring legacy and living culture offer a unique and enriching experience, connecting visitors with a profound history and a resilient community that continues to thrive in the modern world.

27. Georgia O'Keeffe: The famous artist lived in New Mexico and drew inspiration from its landscapes. The renowned artist's former home and studio, Ghost Ranch, is now a retreat and educational center.

28. Zozobra: An annual event in Santa Fe where a giant effigy is burned to symbolize the purging of gloom.

29. Native American Heritage: New Mexico is home to 23 Native American tribes, including the Navajo and Pueblo.

30. Roswell:

Roswell, New Mexico, is internationally famous for its association with UFO lore and the alleged crash of an extraterrestrial spacecraft in 1947. This small city, located in southeastern New Mexico, has embraced its unique place in pop culture history, becoming a hub for UFO enthusiasts and curious tourists alike.

The Roswell Incident began in July 1947, when a rancher named Mac Brazel discovered strange debris scattered across his property near Roswell. Initially reported as a "flying disc," the U.S. military quickly retracted the statement, claiming the debris was from a weather balloon. This sudden change fueled speculation and conspiracy theories about a government cover-up of an alien spacecraft crash.

Over the years, the Roswell Incident has become one of the most enduring and controversial UFO stories. Books, documentaries, and movies have explored the event, contributing to the town's notoriety. The incident also sparked a broader interest in UFOs and extraterrestrial life, leading to the establishment of numerous UFO research organizations.

Today, Roswell capitalizes on its extraterrestrial reputation with the International UFO Museum and Research Center, which attracts thousands of visitors annually. The museum features exhibits on the 1947 incident, UFO sightings, and the broader search for extraterrestrial intelligence. It serves as a focal point for the town's annual UFO Festival, held every July. The festival includes lectures, panel discussions, costume contests, and a parade, drawing enthusiasts from around the world.

Roswell's embrace of its UFO heritage extends to local businesses and attractions. Many shops and restaurants feature alien-themed decor and products, creating a playful and intriguing atmosphere. The city's connection to the skies is further complemented by the Roswell International Air Center, which serves as a commercial and military aviation hub.

Despite its small size, Roswell has made a significant impact on popular culture and continues to be a symbol of humanity's fascination with the unknown.

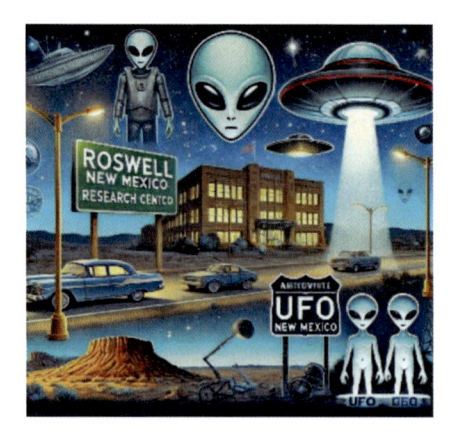

31. Drive-Thru Green Chile: In New Mexico, you can find drive-thru stands selling roasted green chiles, a staple of the local cuisine.

32. Taos Hum: Some residents and visitors in Taos report hearing a mysterious low-frequency humming sound, known as the "Taos Hum."

33. Santa Fe Margarita Trail: A trail featuring over 40 locations where visitors can sample unique margaritas across Santa Fe.

34. Albuquerque International Balloon Fiesta:

The Albuquerque International Balloon Fiesta is the largest hot air balloon festival in the world, held annually in Albuquerque, New Mexico. This spectacular event takes place over nine days in early October, attracting hundreds of balloonists and thousands of spectators from around the globe.

The Balloon Fiesta began in 1972 with just 13 balloons in a shopping mall parking lot. It has since grown into a massive event featuring over 500 balloons, transforming the skies over Albuquerque into a kaleidoscope of colors and shapes. The festival is renowned for its unique Mass Ascensions, where hundreds of balloons launch simultaneously in two waves, creating a breathtaking sight against the backdrop of the Sandia Mountains.

One of the highlights of the Balloon Fiesta is the Special Shape Rodeo, showcasing balloons in a variety of whimsical shapes, from animals and cartoon characters to iconic landmarks. These creative balloons delight visitors of all ages and add an extra layer of fun and excitement to the event.

Another popular attraction is the Balloon Glow, held in the evenings. During this event, balloons are tethered and illuminated from within by their burners, creating a stunning display of glowing colors against the night sky. The Glowdeo, a similar event featuring special shape balloons, adds to the evening's magic.

In addition to ballooning activities, the Fiesta includes a wide range of entertainment options. There are live music performances, chainsaw carving demonstrations, and various competitions, such as the America's Challenge Gas Balloon Race, where teams compete to fly the farthest distance.

Visitors can also enjoy local New Mexican cuisine from numerous food vendors, browse arts and crafts booths, and learn about ballooning history and technology at the Balloon Discovery Center.

The Albuquerque International Balloon Fiesta is a celebration of flight. Its vibrant atmosphere and awe-inspiring displays make it a must-see event for anyone visiting New Mexico.

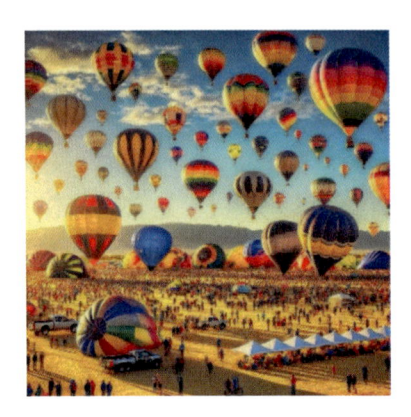

35. Kit Carson: Famous frontiersman who lived in Taos.

36. Conrad Hilton: Founder of the Hilton Hotel chain, born in San Antonio, NM.

37. Railroad Arrival: The Atchison, Topeka, and Santa Fe Railway reached New Mexico in the 1880s, spurring economic growth.

38. Dennis Chavez: First Hispanic U.S. Senator, serving New Mexico from 1935 to 1962.

39. Festival Flamenco Internacional de Alburquerque:

The Festival Flamenco Internacional de Alburquerque, held annually in Albuquerque, New Mexico, is the largest flamenco festival in the United States. This vibrant event, which takes place in June, celebrates the rich cultural heritage and passionate art form of flamenco. It attracts world-renowned flamenco artists and enthusiasts from around the globe.

Founded in 1987 by Eva Encinias, a prominent flamenco dancer and educator, the festival is organized by the National Institute of Flamenco in collaboration with the University of New Mexico. The Festival Flamenco Internacional aims to preserve and promote the traditions of flamenco while fostering artistic exchange and education.

The festival features an impressive lineup of performances by acclaimed flamenco dancers, singers, and musicians. These performances take place at various venues across Albuquerque, including the historic KiMo Theatre and the University of New Mexico's Rodey Theatre. Each show offers a unique experience, showcasing the intricate footwork, soulful singing, and powerful guitar playing that define flamenco.

In addition to performances, the festival offers a comprehensive program of workshops and master classes led by some of the world's top flamenco artists. These classes cater to all skill levels, from beginners to advanced students, providing participants with the opportunity to immerse themselves in the art of flamenco and hone their skills.

The festival also includes lectures, film screenings, and panel discussions that explore the history, culture, and evolution of flamenco. These educational components provide a deeper understanding of the art form and its significance within the global cultural landscape.

The Festival Flamenco Internacional de Alburquerque is a celebration of passion, artistry, and cultural heritage. Its vibrant atmosphere and diverse programming make it an essential event for flamenco aficionados and a highlight of Albuquerque's cultural calendar. The festival's commitment to excellence and education ensures that the legacy of flamenco continues to thrive and inspire future generations.

40. Luminarias and Farolitos: These traditional paper lanterns are used to light up New Mexican towns and cities during Christmas time.

41. Hiking and Outdoor Recreation: New Mexico's diverse landscapes offer numerous opportunities for hiking, mountain biking, and rock climbing.

42. Albuquerque Dukes: A historic Minor League Baseball team that inspired the name of the Isotopes.

43. San Miguel Chapel in Santa Fe:

San Miguel Chapel, located in Santa Fe, New Mexico, is renowned as the oldest church in the United States. Built between 1610 and 1626, this historic adobe structure stands as a testament to the enduring legacy of Spanish colonial architecture and the deep roots of Catholicism in the region.

The chapel was constructed by Tlaxcalan Indians under the direction of Franciscan friars during the early days of Spanish colonization. Its thick adobe walls and wooden vigas (beams) showcase the traditional building techniques of the time, which have helped preserve the structure for over four centuries. Despite renovations and repairs, San Miguel Chapel retains much of its original charm and authenticity.

San Miguel Chapel has served multiple purposes throughout its history. Initially, it was a mission church for the local Native American population. During the Pueblo Revolt of 1680, the chapel was heavily damaged but was later rebuilt when the Spanish returned in 1692. Over the centuries, it has been a place of worship, a cultural landmark, and a symbol of resilience for the Santa Fe community.

Inside the chapel, visitors can admire the beautifully preserved altar screen, or reredos, which dates back to the 18th century. This intricately carved and painted wooden screen features depictions of various saints, reflecting the artistic and religious heritage of the era. The bell of San Miguel, cast in 1356 and brought to the New World by Spanish settlers, is another notable artifact housed within the chapel.

Today, San Miguel Chapel remains an active place of worship and a popular tourist attraction. Its serene atmosphere and historical significance draw visitors from around the world, offering a glimpse into the rich cultural tapestry of Santa Fe and the enduring legacy of its earliest inhabitants.

44. Skiing: Taos Ski Valley is a major ski resort known for its challenging terrain and deep powder.

45. Professional Rodeo: Rodeo is a popular sport with many events held throughout the state.

46. Ralph Kiner: Hall of Fame baseball player, born in Santa Rita.

47. Lowrider Culture in New Mexico:

New Mexico is renowned for its vibrant lowrider culture, which has deep roots in the state's Hispanic communities. Lowriding, a car custom style and lifestyle, emerged in the mid-20th century and has since become an iconic symbol of cultural expression and pride, particularly in cities like Espacola and Albuquerque.

Lowriders are customized cars with hydraulics that allow them to be raised and lowered at the owner's will. These vehicles often feature elaborate paint jobs, chrome details, and plush interiors, transforming them into moving works of art. The intricate designs and craftsmanship reflect the owner's personal style and cultural heritage.

The origins of lowrider culture can be traced back to the post-World War II era when Mexican-American veterans began modifying their cars to cruise slowly and stylishly through their neighborhoods. This practice evolved into a distinct cultural phenomenon that emphasized community, identity, and artistic expression. By the 1970s, lowriding had gained widespread popularity, particularly in the American Southwest.

Espacola, known as the ☐Lowrider Capital of the World,☐ hosts numerous lowrider shows and events, celebrating this unique aspect of New Mexican culture. These gatherings bring together enthusiasts from all over to showcase their cars, share techniques, and celebrate their shared heritage. Albuquerque also has a thriving lowrider scene, with clubs and events that highlight the community's passion for these customized vehicles.

Lowriding is more than just a hobby; it's a lifestyle that encompasses music, fashion, and art. The lowrider community is known for its tight-knit relationships and strong sense of identity. Music, particularly genres like oldies and Chicano rap, often accompanies the cruising culture, creating a vibrant and dynamic atmosphere.

The lowrider culture in New Mexico represents a powerful form of cultural pride and resilience. It celebrates creativity, craftsmanship, and community, while honoring the rich Hispanic heritage of the region. This cultural movement continues to inspire and unite people, making it an integral part of New Mexico's diverse cultural landscape.

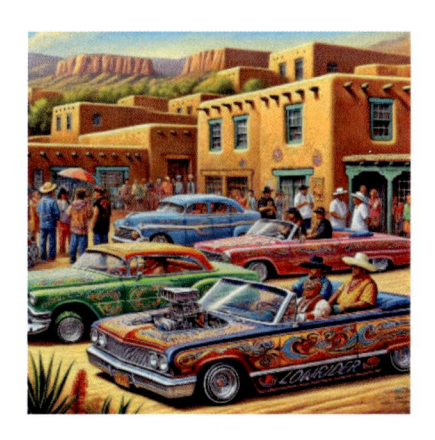

48. Cimarron Canyon: Known for its stunning cliffs, wildlife, and recreational opportunities.

49. Organ Mountains: Located in southern New Mexico, known for their dramatic spires and rugged beauty.

50. Geographical Location: New Mexico is located in the southwestern region of the United States. It is bordered by Colorado to the north, Oklahoma and Texas to the east, Texas and the Mexican states of Chihuahua and Sonora to the south, and Arizona to the west.

The state covers a diverse range of landscapes, including expansive deserts, high plains, and rugged mountains. The Rio Grande, one of North America's longest rivers, flows from north to south through the center of the state, providing vital water resources and supporting agriculture and wildlife. To the north, the Sangre de Cristo Mountains form part of the southern Rockies, offering scenic beauty and recreational opportunities.

New Mexico's capital city, Santa Fe, is located in the north-central part of the state, nestled in the foothills of the Sangre de Cristo Mountains. Albuquerque, the largest city, is situated along the Rio Grande in the central region. The southeastern part of the state features the Chihuahuan Desert, while the southwestern area includes the Gila Wilderness, known for its diverse ecosystems and ancient cliff dwellings.

The state's unique geographical location and varied topography contribute to its rich cultural heritage, blending Native American, Hispanic, and Anglo influences. New Mexico's landscapes are marked by distinctive features such as the White Sands National Park, Carlsbad Caverns National Park, and the volcanic formations of the Valley of Fires. The state's location and natural beauty make it a popular destination for outdoor activities, tourism, and cultural exploration.

07

NEW YORK

1.The Erie Canal:

The Erie Canal is one of the most significant engineering achievements in American history. Completed in 1825, the canal stretches 363 miles from Albany on the Hudson River to Buffalo on Lake Erie, creating a navigable water route from the Atlantic Ocean to the Great Lakes. This waterway played a crucial role in the economic development of New York State and the United States as a whole.

Before the canal, transporting goods between the eastern seaboard and the interior of the country was difficult and expensive. The Erie Canal revolutionized this process by dramatically reducing transportation costs and time. Goods that previously took weeks to transport by road could now be moved in a matter of days, and at a fraction of the cost. This made it much easier for farmers and manufacturers in the interior to access markets in the east, and for imported goods to reach the west.

The construction of the canal was a monumental task, requiring the labor of thousands of workers, many of whom were immigrants. They dug the canal by hand, using picks, shovels, and wheelbarrows. The project faced numerous challenges, including difficult terrain, engineering obstacles, and outbreaks of disease, but it was ultimately completed ahead of schedule and under budget.

The Erie Canal had a profound impact on the growth of New York City, which became a major port and commercial center due to its connection to the interior of the country. It also spurred the development of towns and cities along its route, such as Syracuse, Rochester, and Buffalo. Additionally, the canal played a key role in the westward expansion of the United States, making it easier for settlers to move west and for goods to flow east.

Today, the Erie Canal is a National Historic Landmark and a popular destination for recreational boating and tourism. Its legacy as a transformative infrastructure project continues to be felt in the economic and cultural landscape of New York State and the entire nation.

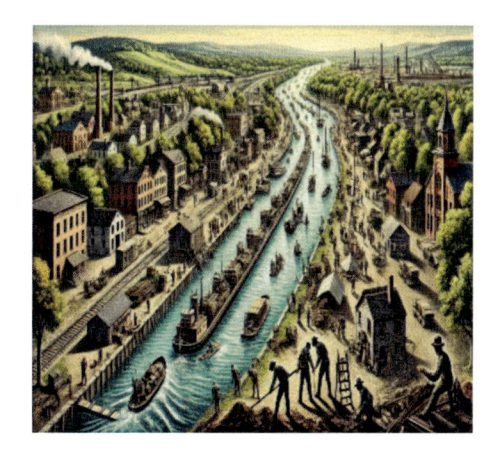

2. First Capital: Kingston was the first capital of New York State in 1777.

3. Largest Solar Telescope: The National Solar Observatory's McMath-Pierce Solar Telescope is located in New York.

4. Women's Rights Movement: Seneca Falls hosted the first women's rights convention in 1848, leading to the Declaration of Sentiments.

5. Ellis Island:

Ellis Island, located in New York Harbor, is often referred to as the "Gateway to America." From 1892 to 1954, it served as the primary immigration station for the United States, processing over 12 million immigrants. This small island played a monumental role in shaping the nation's demographic landscape and remains a powerful symbol of the American immigrant experience.

Ellis Island's operations began on January 1, 1892, when Annie Moore, a young Irish girl, became the first immigrant to pass through its doors. Over the next six decades, the island saw a constant stream of newcomers seeking better opportunities and escaping hardships in their homelands. The peak year was 1907, when over a million immigrants were processed.

Upon arrival, immigrants underwent a rigorous inspection process. This included medical and legal examinations to ensure they were fit to enter the country. The process could take hours or even days, and those who were found to have health issues or other problems could be detained or sent back to their countries of origin. Despite these challenges, the majority of immigrants passed through successfully, starting new lives in the United States.

Ellis Island's role as an immigration station ended in 1954, and it eventually fell into disrepair. However, in the 1980s, a major restoration project transformed the island into a museum dedicated to the history of immigration in America. The Ellis Island Immigration Museum, which opened in 1990, now features exhibits, artifacts, and interactive displays that tell the stories of the millions of people who passed through its halls.

Ellis Island is also home to the American Family Immigration History Center, where visitors can search for records of their ancestors who came through the island. This connection to personal and family history makes Ellis Island a deeply meaningful place for many Americans.

Today, Ellis Island is part of the Statue of Liberty National Monument and continues to be a symbol of hope and new beginnings. It stands as a testament to the diverse and multicultural heritage of the United States, reminding us of the countless journeys that have shaped the nation.

6. Oldest National Park: Saratoga National Historical Park, established in 1938, commemorates the American victory in the Revolutionary War.

7. Niagara Falls: One of the most powerful waterfalls in North America. It spans the border between the province of Ontario in Canada and New York Stat and it generates over 4 million kilowatts of electricity.

8. NASA Space Shuttle: The Intrepid Sea, Air & Space Museum in NYC hosts the Space Shuttle Enterprise.

9. Jazz Music: Harlem is a historical epicenter for jazz, hosting icons like Duke Ellington and Louis Armstrong.

10. Gilboa Fossil Forest:

The Gilboa Fossil Forest, located in the Catskill Mountains of New York, is one of the most significant paleontological discoveries in the world. Dating back approximately 385 million years to the Devonian period, it is considered one of the oldest fossilized forests ever discovered. This ancient forest provides crucial insights into the evolution of early terrestrial ecosystems.

Discovered in the 1920s during the construction of the Gilboa Dam, the fossil forest was initially thought to consist primarily of fossilized tree stumps. However, further excavations in the early 21st century revealed a more complex and diverse array of plant life. The forest was dominated by primitive tree-like plants known as "Eospermatopteris" and featured a variety of other flora, including early ferns and other vascular plants.

The significance of the Gilboa Fossil Forest lies in its ability to offer a window into a time when life on land was still in its early stages. The preserved remains of these ancient plants provide valuable information about the structure and composition of early forests, as well as the environmental conditions in which they thrived. This helps scientists understand how plants adapted to life on land and how early terrestrial ecosystems functioned.

Today, the Gilboa Fossil Forest is a protected site, and many of its fossil specimens are housed in museums around the world, including the New York State Museum in Albany. Visitors to the region can explore the Gilboa Museum, which showcases some of the most significant finds from the fossil forest and offers educational exhibits about the Devonian period and the history of paleontology.

The Gilboa Fossil Forest remains a testament to the rich geological and paleontological heritage of New York State, providing a fascinating glimpse into the ancient past and the early evolution of life on land.

11. Museums for Everything: NYC has museums dedicated to unusual topics, like the Museum of Food and Drink and the Morbid Anatomy Museum.

12. Safety Pin: Walter Hunt invented this handy item in New York City in 1849.

13. Lin-Manuel Miranda: Composer and playwright, creator of "Hamilton," born in New York City in 1980.

14. Fort Ticonderoga:

Fort Ticonderoga, located on the shores of Lake Champlain in New York, is a historic site of great importance in American history. Originally built by the French in 1755 during the French and Indian War, the fort was known as Fort Carillon. It played a crucial role in several key military engagements and is now a popular destination for history enthusiasts.

During the French and Indian War, Fort Carillon was a strategic stronghold for the French, allowing them to control access to the waterways between Canada and the American colonies. In 1758, the fort was the site of the Battle of Carillon, where a significantly outnumbered French force successfully defended the fort against a larger British army.

The fort's significance continued into the American Revolutionary War. In 1775, the Green Mountain Boys, led by Ethan Allen and Benedict Arnold, captured Fort Ticonderoga from the British in a surprise attack. This victory was crucial because it provided the Continental Army with much-needed artillery, which was later used in the Siege of Boston.

In 1777, the British, under General John Burgoyne, recaptured Fort Ticonderoga during their campaign to gain control of the Hudson River Valley. However, the fort was abandoned by the British in 1781, and it fell into disrepair over the following decades.

In the early 20th century, Fort Ticonderoga was restored by private owners who recognized its historical significance. Today, it operates as a museum and historical site, offering visitors a chance to explore its well-preserved structures and learn about its storied past. The fort hosts reenactments, educational programs, and special events that bring history to life.

Fort Ticonderoga remains a symbol of the strategic and military struggles that shaped the early history of the United States. Its preservation allows future generations to connect with the nation's past and gain a deeper understanding of the events that influenced the course of American history.

15. Dancing Traffic Light: There's a traffic light in Canajoharie that dances when the light changes.

16. Ghost Subway Stations: Abandoned stations like the City Hall Station are hidden beneath New York City.

17. Times Square Ball: The New Year's Eve ball drop in Times Square has been a tradition since 1907.

18. Mysterious Road: The "Gravity Hill" in Richfield Springs appears to defy gravity, making cars roll uphill.

<u>19. North Brother Island:</u>

North Brother Island is a small, uninhabited island located in the East River between the Bronx and Rikers Island. It has a fascinating and somewhat eerie history that has left it shrouded in mystery and intrigue. The island was first developed in 1885 as the site of the Riverside Hospital, which was initially established to quarantine and treat patients with contagious diseases such as smallpox, tuberculosis, and typhoid fever.

One of the most infamous residents of North Brother Island was Mary Mallon, better known as "Typhoid Mary." She was a cook who became the first person in the United States identified as an asymptomatic carrier of the typhoid fever pathogen. Mallon was confined to the island for several years until her death in 1938 to prevent her from spreading the disease.

In 1904, North Brother Island was the site of one of the deadliest maritime disasters in American history. The General Slocum, a passenger steamboat, caught fire and sank near the island, resulting in the deaths of over 1,000 people. This tragedy further cemented the island's place in New York City's lore.

After World War II, the island was repurposed to house returning veterans and, later, as a treatment center for adolescent drug addicts in the 1950s. However, the program was unsuccessful, and the island was abandoned in the 1960s.

Today, North Brother Island is off-limits to the public and has become a bird sanctuary, particularly for herons. The ruins of the hospital and other buildings remain, slowly being reclaimed by nature. The island stands as a haunting reminder of its storied past, a place where history and nature intersect in a unique and poignant way.

20. Gay Rights Movement: The Stonewall Riots in 1969 in Greenwich Village marked the beginning of the gay rights movement.

21. Dutch Settlement: The establishment of New Amsterdam by the Dutch in 1624, which later became New York City.

22. Lady Gaga: Singer and actress, born in Manhattan in 1986.

23. Rooftop Farms: Brooklyn Grange operates the world's largest rooftop soil farms.

24. New York City's Subway System:

New York City's subway system is one of the oldest, largest, and most iconic public transit systems in the world. Opened in 1904, the subway has grown to encompass 472 stations and over 665 miles of track, serving millions of riders every day. The subway is a vital part of the city's infrastructure and a symbol of its urban dynamism.

The idea for an underground transit system in New York City was first proposed in the 19th century, as the city's streets became increasingly congested with horse-drawn carriages and elevated trains. The construction of the subway was a monumental engineering feat, involving the excavation of deep tunnels beneath the bustling city. The first line, known as the IRT (Interborough Rapid Transit), ran from City Hall in Lower Manhattan to 145th Street in Harlem.

The subway system expanded rapidly in the early 20th century, with the construction of new lines and the integration of previously separate systems. This expansion helped shape the city's growth, making it easier for people to live farther from their workplaces and travel quickly across the boroughs. The subway played a crucial role in the development of neighborhoods and the city's economy.

Over the years, the subway has seen numerous changes and improvements, from the introduction of electric trains to the implementation of modern safety and communication systems. Despite these advancements, the system has faced challenges, including financial difficulties, maintenance issues, and the impact of natural disasters like Hurricane Sandy.

Today, the New York City subway remains an essential part of daily life for millions of residents and visitors. It is a microcosm of the city's diversity, with people from all walks of life sharing the same space as they commute to work, school, and beyond. The subway's iconic stations, unique architecture, and vibrant art installations make it more than just a mode of transportation; it is an integral part of New York City's identity and culture.

25. 9/11 Attacks: Terrorist attacks on the World Trade Center in New York City on September 11, 2001.

26. The Invention of Air Conditioning:

Air conditioning, a technology we often take for granted today, was invented by Willis Carrier in 1902. This groundbreaking invention originated in Buffalo, New York, and revolutionized both industrial processes and everyday life.

Willis Carrier, a young engineer, was tasked with solving a problem at a Brooklyn printing plant. The high humidity levels during the summer were causing the paper to wrinkle and the ink to smudge. Carrier developed a system that used coils to cool the air and remove moisture, effectively controlling both temperature and humidity. This system, known as the "Apparatus for Treating Air," became the world's first modern air conditioner.

Carrier's invention had immediate and far-reaching impacts. Initially, it was used in industrial settings, such as printing plants and textile mills, where controlling humidity and temperature was crucial for product quality. However, it didn't take long for the technology to spread to other sectors. Theaters, department stores, and office buildings soon adopted air conditioning, transforming the way people worked and shopped. The first air-conditioned movie theater opened in 1925, offering a cool respite from the summer heat and boosting attendance.

Air conditioning played a significant role in the development of modern architecture and urban planning. It enabled the construction of skyscrapers with sealed windows and large, open floor plans, as these buildings could now be efficiently cooled. It also facilitated population growth in hot climates, making regions like the American South and Southwest more habitable and economically viable.

Today, air conditioning is a ubiquitous part of modern life, improving comfort and productivity across the globe. Willis Carrier's invention not only solved an immediate problem but also laid the foundation for advancements in climate control that continue to benefit society.

27. Billy Joel: Singer-songwriter, known as the "Piano Man," born in the Bronx in 1949.

28. Subway Showers: In New York City, you can find subway stations where rainwater leaks create unexpected indoor showers.

29. Cornelius Vanderbilt: Industrialist and philanthropist, made significant contributions to railroads and shipping.

30. The Invention of the Elevator Brake:

The invention of the elevator brake by Elisha Otis in 1852 was a pivotal moment in the history of urban development and architecture. Before this invention, elevators were considered dangerous and unreliable, limiting their use primarily to freight rather than passengers.

Elisha Otis was a mechanic and inventor who recognized the need for a safer elevator system. At the time, elevators were powered by steam and hoisted by ropes, which could easily break and cause the elevator to plummet. Otis's breakthrough came with his design of a safety brake that would automatically engage if the hoisting rope broke. His device used a spring mechanism to push a series of metal teeth into the guide rails of the elevator shaft, halting the fall and preventing a catastrophic accident.

To demonstrate the effectiveness of his invention, Otis conducted a dramatic public demonstration at the 1854 New York World's Fair in the Crystal Palace. Standing on an elevated platform, he ordered the hoisting rope to be cut, and as the platform began to fall, the safety brake engaged, stopping the descent and leaving Otis unharmed. This demonstration captured the public's imagination and established the safety and reliability of his elevator brake.

Otis's invention revolutionized the construction industry and paved the way for the development of skyscrapers. With safe and reliable elevators, buildings could be constructed taller than ever before, transforming city skylines and urban living. The elevator brake made vertical transportation feasible and practical, allowing for the efficient use of space in densely populated urban areas.

Today, the Otis Elevator Company, founded by Elisha Otis, remains a leading manufacturer of elevators and escalators. The principles behind Otis's safety brake continue to be integral to modern elevator design, ensuring the safety of millions of passengers every day. Elisha Otis's invention not only made skyscrapers possible but also played a crucial role in shaping the modern city.

31. Alexander Hamilton: Founding Father and first Secretary of the Treasury, lived and worked in New York City.

32. Underground Park: The Lowline is an abandoned trolley terminal being converted into an underground park with natural sunlight.

33. Lakes on Skyscrapers: Some NYC skyscrapers have artificial lakes on their rooftops for cooling purposes.

34. The Invention of the Wireless Remote Control:

The invention of the wireless remote control can be traced back to Nikola Tesla, a pioneering inventor and electrical engineer who conducted much of his groundbreaking work in New York. In 1898, Tesla demonstrated his revolutionary invention at Madison Square Garden in New York City, astonishing the audience with a radio-controlled boat.

Tesla's invention was a small, radio-controlled boat that he referred to as a "teleautomaton." The boat could be maneuvered from a distance using radio waves, which Tesla controlled with a handheld device. This was the first instance of a device being remotely operated without any physical connection, a concept that was far ahead of its time.

During his demonstration, Tesla showed the boat moving forward, backward, left, and right, all controlled by his remote device. The audience was amazed, and many could not believe what they were witnessing. Some even speculated that Tesla was using magic or telepathy to control the boat. However, Tesla explained that his invention worked through the transmission of radio waves, which he had been studying and experimenting with extensively.

Tesla's invention laid the groundwork for the development of modern wireless technology. The principles behind his remote control are the foundation for countless devices we use today, from television remotes to drones and other advanced technologies. His work in radio control also paved the way for the development of other wireless communication technologies, including Wi-Fi and Bluetooth.

Despite the initial skepticism, Tesla's invention eventually gained recognition for its ingenuity and potential. Today, the wireless remote control is a ubiquitous part of modern life, enabling convenience and control in numerous applications. Tesla's work remains a testament to his visionary genius and his lasting impact on technology.

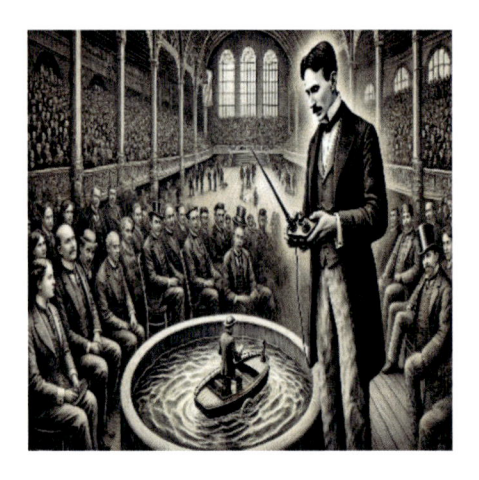

35. Blackout of 1977: Major power outage in New York City that led to widespread looting and arson.

36. Eleanor Roosevelt: First Lady, diplomat, and activist, born in New York City.

37. George Washington: First President of the United States, inaugurated in New York City in 1789.

38. Wall Street Crash: The stock market crash of 1929, marking the beginning of the Great Depression.

39. The Secret Apartment in the Torch of the Statue of Liberty:

The Statue of Liberty, an iconic symbol of freedom and democracy, holds many secrets within its towering structure. One of the most intriguing secrets is the existence of a small, hidden apartment inside the statue's torch. This apartment, located in the uppermost part of the statue, was originally intended for a specific and practical purpose.

When the statue was designed by French sculptor Frйdйric Auguste Bartholdi and built with the assistance of engineer Gustave Eiffel, the torch was equipped with a balcony that offered a panoramic view of New York Harbor. Within the torch itself, there is a small room that was intended to serve as a storage and maintenance area. This space provided access to the torch for maintenance workers and for Bartholdi himself.

During the statue's construction, Bartholdi used the apartment as a workspace and observation point. It offered a unique vantage point for overseeing the final stages of the statue's assembly and installation. The room was outfitted with a small bed, table, and chairs, making it a functional space for short stays.

However, the torch and its apartment have been closed to the public since 1916, following an explosion on nearby Black Tom Island, which caused structural damage. The torch was subsequently deemed unsafe for visitors, and access has been restricted ever since.

Despite its closure, the secret apartment in the torch remains a fascinating aspect of the Statue of Liberty's history. It adds an element of mystery and intrigue to the already captivating story of the statue. While visitors can no longer access the torch, the knowledge of this hidden room continues to inspire curiosity and wonder about the statue's many hidden facets.

40. Kodak Camera: Invented by George Eastman in 1888, revolutionizing photography.

41. Tiny House: The Skinny House in Mamaroneck is just 10 feet wide and is one of the narrowest homes in the world.

42. Microclimate: Manhattan creates its own weather, with slightly warmer temperatures than the surrounding areas.

43. Spike Lee:

Spike Lee, born Shelton Jackson Lee on March 20, 1957, in Atlanta, Georgia, and raised in Brooklyn, New York, is a prolific filmmaker, writer, director, and producer. Known for his provocative and socially conscious films, Lee has become a significant figure in American cinema, addressing issues of race, class, and identity with a distinctive and powerful voice.

Lee's interest in filmmaking began at an early age, and he pursued his passion by studying at Morehouse College and later at New

York University's Tisch School of the Arts. His breakthrough came with the release of "She's Gotta Have It" in 1986, a low-budget film that received critical acclaim and established Lee as a talented and innovative filmmaker.

One of Lee's most influential films is "Do the Right Thing" (1989), which explores racial tensions in a Brooklyn neighborhood on a hot summer day. The film was both praised and criticized for its unflinching portrayal of race relations, sparking conversations and debates about the state of race in America. "Do the Right Thing" received two Academy Award nominations and has been preserved in the National Film Registry for its cultural significance.

Throughout his career, Lee has continued to tackle challenging and important themes. Films like "Malcolm X" (1992), "25th Hour" (2002), and "BlacKkKlansman" (2018) have cemented his reputation as a filmmaker who is unafraid to confront social issues head-on. "BlacKkKlansman," which tells the true story of an African American police officer infiltrating the Ku Klux Klan, won the Grand Prix at the Cannes Film Festival and earned Lee his first Academy Award for Best Adapted Screenplay.

In addition to his feature films, Lee has directed documentaries, music videos, and commercials, showcasing his versatility and creative range. He is also a professor at NYU's Tisch School of the Arts, where he mentors the next generation of filmmakers.

Spike Lee's impact on cinema and culture is profound. His work challenges audiences to think critically about social issues and has paved the way for more diverse voices in the film industry. Lee's legacy as a filmmaker and cultural icon continues to inspire and provoke thought, making him a pivotal figure in modern American cinema.

44. Toilet Paper: Invented by Joseph Gayetty in 1857, it was first marketed in New York.

45. Tug-of-War Bridge: In 1933, the George Washington Bridge was the site of a real tug-of-war between New York and New Jersey tugboats.

46. Pizza Rat: A famous internet sensation, "Pizza Rat" was a rat filmed dragging a slice of pizza down the stairs of a subway station.

47. The Woodstock Festival:

The Woodstock Festival, held from August 15 to 18, 1969, in Bethel, New York, is one of the most iconic events in music history. Billed as "An Aquarian Exposition: 3 Days of Peace & Music," Woodstock became a defining moment for the counterculture movement of the 1960s and a symbol of the era's spirit of peace, love, and music.

Originally planned to accommodate around 50,000 attendees, the festival ended up attracting over 400,000 people, far exceeding expectations. The influx of people created logistical challenges, including traffic jams, food shortages, and inadequate sanitation facilities. Despite these issues, the festival is remembered for its peaceful atmosphere and the sense of community among attendees.

Woodstock featured performances by some of the most influential musicians of the time, including Jimi Hendrix, Janis Joplin, The Who, and Jefferson Airplane. Hendrix's rendition of "The Star-Spangled Banner," played on the final morning of the festival, became one of the most iconic moments in rock history. His electric guitar interpretation of the national anthem was both a musical innovation and a powerful statement on the social and political issues of the time.

The festival also highlighted the power of music as a unifying force. Despite the adverse conditions, the spirit of cooperation and camaraderie prevailed. The event was free of significant violence, and the collective experience fostered a sense of hope and possibility among the attendees.

Woodstock's legacy extends beyond the music and the event itself. It inspired numerous other music festivals and left an indelible mark on popular culture. The festival was documented in the 1970 film "Woodstock," which won an Academy Award for Best Documentary Feature, further cementing its place in history.

Today, Woodstock is celebrated as a landmark event that encapsulated the ideals and aspirations of a generation. It remains a powerful symbol of the enduring impact of music and cultural expression in shaping societal values and inspiring change.

48. Pfizer: A pharmaceutical giant headquartered in NYC.

49. Statehood: New York State joined the Union on July 26, 1788. It was the 11th state to ratify the United States Constitution.

50. Geographical Location: New York State is located in the northeastern region of the United States. It shares a northern border with Canada, specifically the provinces of Quebec and Ontario. To the east, New York is bordered by Vermont, Massachusetts, and Connecticut. The southern boundary of New York is shared with New Jersey and Pennsylvania. The state also has a coastal boundary along the Atlantic Ocean, with Long Island extending into the ocean, creating a significant part of its southeastern geography.

New York State is known for its diverse landscapes, which include the Adirondack Mountains in the northeast, the Catskill Mountains in the southeast, and the Appalachian Plateau extending into the southern tier. The state is also home to the Great Lakes, with Lake

Ontario forming part of its northern border and Lake Erie touching its western edge. The Hudson River runs from the northern part of the state down to New York City, which is situated on the southeastern tip of the state, along the Atlantic coast. This geographical diversity makes New York State a unique blend of urban, suburban, and rural environments.

08

NORTH CAROLINA

1. The Wright Brothers

The Wright Brothers, Orville and Wilbur Wright, are credited with inventing and building the world's first successful powered airplane. Their historic flight took place on December 17, 1903, at Kill Devil Hills near Kitty Hawk, North Carolina. This monumental event marked the beginning of the aviation era and forever changed the way humans travel and perceive distance.

Orville and Wilbur Wright were born in Dayton, Ohio, where they initially developed an interest in flight. They conducted extensive research and experiments, building on the work of earlier aviation pioneers. The brothers meticulously studied aerodynamics, control systems, and propulsion, leading to several successful glider flights before attempting powered flight.

In 1903, they traveled to the remote sand dunes of Kitty Hawk due to its steady winds and soft landing surfaces, ideal for testing their flying machines. The Wright Flyer, their powered aircraft, was constructed of spruce wood and muslin fabric, featuring a 12-horsepower engine and twin propellers. On that historic December day, Orville piloted the first flight, which lasted 12 seconds and covered 120 feet. They made three more flights that day, with the longest covering 852 feet in 59 seconds, piloted by Wilbur.

The Wright Brothers' success was not just a result of their engineering skills but also their methodical approach to problem-solving and relentless perseverance. Their achievements paved the way for modern aviation, leading to advancements in transportation, communication, and warfare. The Wright Brothers' legacy is commemorated at the Wright Brothers National Memorial in Kill Devil Hills, where visitors can learn about their pioneering work and witness a replica of the original Wright Flyer.

2. First English Colony: The Lost Colony of Roanoke, established in 1587, was the first English settlement in America.

3. First State University: The University of North Carolina at Chapel Hill, chartered in 1789, is the oldest public university in the United States.

4. Civil War: North Carolina was a key battleground during the Civil War, with significant battles such as Bentonville.

5. Halifax Resolves:

The Halifax Resolves was a pivotal document in American history, representing the first official action by a colony calling for independence from Britain. Adopted on April 12, 1776, by the Fourth Provincial Congress of North Carolina, the Halifax Resolves was a bold step towards the formation of a new, independent nation.

During the early months of 1776, the sentiment for independence was growing among the American colonies. The citizens of North Carolina were particularly outspoken against British rule, influenced by the oppressive measures and harsh policies imposed by the Crown. In response, North Carolina's provincial congress convened in Halifax, a small town that had become a center of revolutionary activity.

The Halifax Resolves was drafted by a committee led by Cornelius Harnett, a prominent patriot and leader in the colony. The document stated that North Carolina's delegates to the Continental Congress were authorized to concur with other colonies in declaring independence and forming foreign alliances. This was a significant move, as it demonstrated a unified desire for freedom and self-governance.

The adoption of the Halifax Resolves set a precedent for other colonies. It inspired similar actions and declarations of independence, culminating in the Continental Congress's adoption of the Declaration of Independence on July 4, 1776. The Resolves also bolstered the morale of American patriots, reinforcing their commitment to the cause of liberty.

Today, the Halifax Resolves is celebrated as a crucial milestone in the path to American independence. Halifax, North Carolina, honors this legacy with the Historic Halifax State Historic Site, where visitors can explore restored buildings, exhibits, and reenactments that bring the revolutionary era to life. The annual Halifax Day celebration commemorates the adoption of the Resolves, reminding us of the courage and vision of those who fought for American independence.

6. Research Triangle Park: One of the largest research parks in the world, located between Raleigh, Durham, and Chapel Hill.

7. Highest Peak: Mount Mitchell, at 6,684 feet, is the highest peak east of the Mississippi River.

8. Hurricane Alley: The state frequently experiences hurricanes, with notable storms like Hurricane Fran in 1996.

9. Biltmore Estate: The largest privately-owned house in the United States, located in Asheville.

10. Duke University:

Duke University, located in Durham, North Carolina, is one of the most prestigious private universities in the United States. Established in 1838 as Brown's Schoolhouse in the town of Trinity, it was later renamed Union Institute Academy in 1841, Normal College in 1851, and then Trinity College in 1859. The university moved to Durham in 1892, thanks to the generous donations from Washington Duke, a wealthy tobacco industrialist and philanthropist. In 1924, Trinity College was renamed Duke University to honor Washington Duke and his family's substantial contributions to the institution.

Duke University is renowned for its rigorous academics, cutting-edge research, and strong emphasis on interdisciplinary studies. The university comprises ten schools and colleges, with notable programs in law, business, engineering, medicine, and public policy. Duke's medical school, nursing school, and hospital are consistently ranked among the top in the nation.

The campus is known for its stunning Gothic architecture, with the Duke Chapel being a central landmark. Completed in 1935, the chapel's 210-foot tower is an iconic feature of the university. The Sarah P. Duke Gardens, covering 55 acres, provide a beautiful and tranquil space for students and visitors to explore.

Duke is also recognized for its strong athletic programs, particularly its men's basketball team. Coached by the legendary Mike Krzyzewski, the Blue Devils have won multiple NCAA championships and produced numerous NBA players. The intense rivalry between Duke and the University of North Carolina at Chapel Hill is one of the most storied in college sports.

Duke University's commitment to research, academic excellence, and community engagement has made it a leader in higher education. It attracts students and faculty from around the world, fostering a diverse and dynamic academic environment.

11. Bluegrass Music: North Carolina is a significant center for bluegrass music, with numerous festivals and events.

12. Furniture Capital: High Point is known as the "Furniture Capital of the World" and hosts a major international furniture market.

13. State Fair: The North Carolina State Fair in Raleigh is one of the largest and oldest state fairs in the country.

14. The Great Smoky Mountains:

The Great Smoky Mountains, a subrange of the Appalachian Mountains, straddle the border between North Carolina and Tennessee. This majestic mountain range is renowned for its stunning biodiversity, rich cultural history, and breathtaking natural beauty. The Great Smoky Mountains National Park, established in 1934, is the most visited national park in the United States, drawing millions of visitors each year.

The name "Smoky" comes from the natural fog that often hangs over the range, creating a misty, smoky appearance. This phenomenon is due to the vegetation exhaling water vapor, which contains organic compounds that scatter blue light from the sky. The park encompasses over 500,000 acres of lush forests, cascading waterfalls, and more than 800 miles of hiking trails.

The Great Smoky Mountains are home to an incredible array of plant and animal life. The park contains over 19,000 documented species, with estimates of up to 100,000 species that may live within its boundaries. This includes black bears, white-tailed deer, and a variety of bird species, making it a paradise for wildlife enthusiasts and researchers.

The cultural history of the Great Smoky Mountains is equally rich. The region was originally inhabited by the Cherokee people, who have lived in the area for thousands of years. The park preserves numerous historical structures, including log cabins, barns, churches, and grist mills, providing a glimpse into the lives of early European settlers.

Visitors to the Great Smoky Mountains can enjoy a wide range of recreational activities, such as hiking, camping, fishing, and horseback riding. Popular trails include the Appalachian Trail, which passes through the park, and Clingmans Dome, the highest point in the Smokies at 6,643 feet, offering panoramic views of the surrounding landscape.

The Great Smoky Mountains' combination of natural splendor and cultural heritage makes it a cherished destination for nature lovers and history buffs alike. Its preservation as a national park ensures that future generations can continue to experience its wonders.

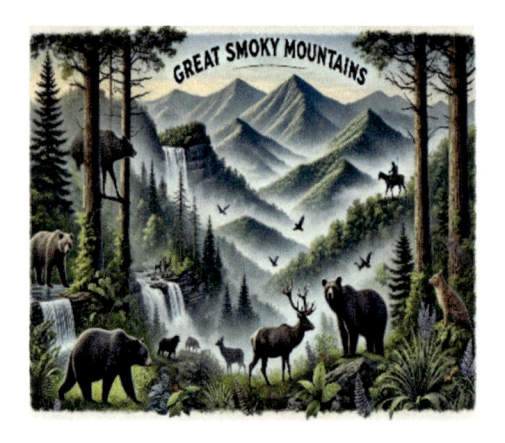

15. Andy Griffith Show: The fictional town of Mayberry was based on Mount Airy, Andy Griffith's hometown.

16. Tryon Palace: The first permanent state capitol, located in New Bern.

17. Outer Banks: A chain of barrier islands known for their natural beauty and historic sites.

18. Carolina Panthers: NFL team based in Charlotte.

19. Venus Flytrap: North Carolina's Carnivorous Marvel

One of the most fascinating plants in the world, the Venus flytrap, calls North Carolina its native home. Found primarily in the subtropical wetlands of this state, especially around Wilmington, this plant is a true wonder of nature. Unlike most plants that rely solely on photosynthesis, the Venus flytrap has developed a unique adaptation to thrive in nutrient-poor soil: it is carnivorous.

The Venus flytrap has specialized leaves that act like jaws, complete with hair-like sensors on their inner surfaces. When an unsuspecting insect touches these sensors twice within 20 seconds, the trap snaps shut in less than a second, enclosing the prey. The plant then secretes digestive enzymes to break down the insect's body, absorbing essential nutrients such as nitrogen and phosphorus, which are scarce in its native soil. This process can take about 5 to 12 days, depending on the size of the insect and environmental conditions.

Interestingly, the Venus flytrap's mechanism is highly energy-efficient. If a non-nutritive object like a pebble triggers the trap, it will open within a day, conserving its energy for actual prey. This adaptation ensures that the plant doesn't waste resources on inedible items. The entire trapping process is an incredible example of nature's ingenuity, showcasing how life can adapt in remarkable ways to survive in challenging environments.

In North Carolina, conservation efforts are crucial as this unique plant faces threats from habitat destruction and poaching. Visitors to the state can see these amazing plants in their natural habitat at places like the Green Swamp Preserve. The Venus flytrap stands as a symbol of the delicate balance within ecosystems and the incredible diversity of life found in North Carolina.

20. Textiles: North Carolina has a long history in the textile industry, particularly in cities like Greensboro and High Point.

21. Banking: Charlotte is the second-largest banking center in the United States, home to Bank of America.

22. Blue Ridge Parkway: A scenic highway that runs through the Blue Ridge Mountains, famous for its stunning views.

23. Tobacco: Historically a major producer of tobacco, with companies like R.J. Reynolds based in the state.

24. The Birth of Pepsi: North Carolina's Fizzy Legacy

In 1893, in the small town of New Bern, North Carolina, a young pharmacist named Caleb Bradham invented a drink that would become a global sensation: Pepsi-Cola. Originally named "Brad's Drink," this refreshing beverage was intended to aid digestion and boost energy, a common need for the people of that era. Bradham combined carbonated water, sugar, vanilla, rare oils, pepsin, and kola nuts to create his concoction.

The drink quickly gained popularity, prompting Bradham to rename it "Pepsi-Cola" in 1898, reflecting its ingredients and intended benefits. The name "Pepsi" comes from "pepsin," an enzyme that aids digestion, though pepsin was never actually an ingredient in the drink. The "Cola" part was due to the kola nuts used in the recipe.

Bradham's pharmacy became a local hotspot, and the success of Pepsi-Cola grew rapidly. By 1902, Bradham established the Pepsi-Cola Company, and the drink began to be bottled and distributed more widely. Despite facing stiff competition from Coca-Cola, Pepsi's unique flavor and marketing strategies helped it carve out a significant niche in the burgeoning soft drink market.

However, Bradham's fortunes took a downturn during World War I due to sugar rationing and price fluctuations, leading to the bankruptcy of his company in 1923. The brand changed hands several times before being revitalized in the 1930s by Charles Guth, who restructured the company and pioneered innovative marketing strategies.

Today, Pepsi is one of the world's leading soft drink brands. Visitors to New Bern can explore the Birthplace of Pepsi-Cola store, which stands on the original site of Bradham's pharmacy, offering a nostalgic glimpse into the humble beginnings of this iconic beverage.

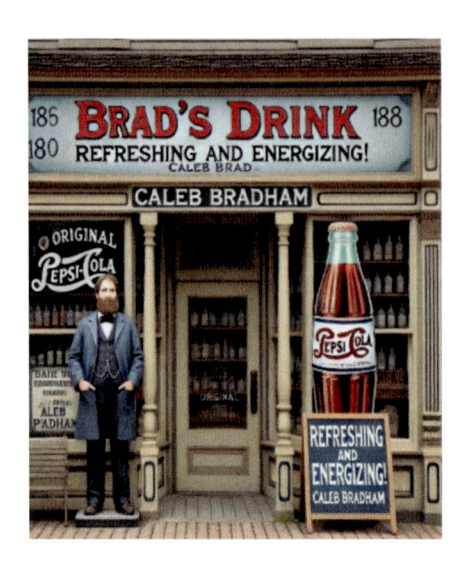

25. Krispy Kreme: Founded in Winston-Salem, known for its iconic doughnuts.

26. The Edenton Tea Party: A Bold Stand for Liberty

In the early days of American resistance against British rule, one of the most notable acts of defiance took place in the small town of Edenton, North Carolina. On October 25, 1774, 51 women from Edenton gathered at the home of Elizabeth King to stage what would become known as the Edenton Tea Party. This event was one of the first organized political actions by women in American history, showcasing their resolve and commitment to the cause of liberty.

The women of Edenton, led by Penelope Barker, were inspired by the Boston Tea Party, where American colonists protested against the Tea Act by dumping British tea into Boston Harbor. However, the Edenton Tea Party was unique because it was a peaceful demonstration. The women signed a resolution declaring their boycott of British tea and other goods, vowing to support the American cause. This act of defiance was not just about tea; it was about standing up against taxation without representation and asserting their rights.

Their bold action received international attention, and while it was ridiculed in British newspapers, it demonstrated the widespread support for the American cause and the crucial role women played in the struggle for independence. The Edenton Tea Party highlighted the spirit of unity and resistance that would eventually lead to the formation of a new nation.

Today, visitors to Edenton can explore the town's rich history, including the site where the Edenton Tea Party took place. A historical marker commemorates this significant event, reminding us of the courage and determination of these pioneering women who helped shape the course of American history.

27. First Mini-Golf Course: The first miniature golf course, named "Thistle Dhu," was built in Fayetteville in 1916.

28. Digital Display: IBM in Research Triangle Park developed the first high-speed printer in the 1950s.

29. Michael Jordan: Born in Brooklyn but raised in Wilmington, he is considered the greatest basketball player of all time.

30. The Cape Hatteras Lighthouse: A Beacon of Safety and History

Standing tall on the Outer Banks of North Carolina, the Cape Hatteras Lighthouse is one of the most iconic landmarks in the United States. Completed in 1870, it was built to guide sailors through the treacherous waters known as the "Graveyard of the Atlantic," where numerous ships had met their doom on the shifting sandbars and violent storms. The Cape Hatteras Lighthouse was the first in the U.S. to use automated technology.

With its distinctive black-and-white spiral pattern, it is the tallest brick lighthouse in North America, standing at 210 feet. Its powerful light, which can be seen from over 20 miles away, has been a beacon of safety for mariners for over a century. The lighthouse's history is rich with tales of daring rescues, shipwrecks, and the relentless power of the sea.

In the late 20th century, the lighthouse faced a new threat: erosion. The encroaching ocean was threatening to topple this historic structure. In 1999, a remarkable engineering feat was undertaken to move the lighthouse 2,900 feet inland to protect it from the advancing shoreline. This delicate and complex operation was successful, preserving the lighthouse for future generations.

Today, the Cape Hatteras Lighthouse is a popular tourist destination, where visitors can climb its 257 steps to the top for a breathtaking view of the Atlantic Ocean and the surrounding landscape. The lighthouse serves as a powerful symbol of resilience and ingenuity, reflecting the rich maritime heritage of North.

31. Statehood: North Carolina was the 12th state to join the Union on November 21, 1789.

32. First State Capitol: New Bern served as the first state capital until Raleigh was established as the permanent capital in 1792

33. Trail of Tears: The Cherokee Nation's forced removal in the 1830s included routes through North Carolina.

34. Old Salem: A Living History Museum

Nestled in Winston-Salem, North Carolina, Old Salem is a meticulously preserved historic district that offers a fascinating glimpse into 18th and 19th-century Moravian life. Founded in 1766 by Moravian settlers, a Protestant group from present-day Czech Republic, Old Salem was designed as a self-sufficient community, where residents lived according to their religious principles and communal values.

The Moravians were skilled craftsmen and farmers, and their settlement quickly became known for its high-quality goods and innovative practices. The town's layout, with its carefully planned streets and buildings, reflects the Moravian emphasis on community and order. Key structures include the Single Brothers' House, the Home Moravian Church, and the Salem Tavern, where George Washington once stayed during his Southern tour in 1791.

Old Salem's living history museum brings the past to life through interactive exhibits, costumed interpreters, and hands-on activities. Visitors can watch blacksmiths, potters, and bakers at work, just as they would have in the 18th century. The museum also highlights the contributions of African Americans, both enslaved and free, who played a significant role in the community's development.

One of the standout features of Old Salem is the Miksch Garden and House, where visitors can see heirloom crops being grown using traditional methods. This garden is a testament to the Moravians' agricultural expertise and their commitment to sustainability.

Old Salem is more than just a collection of historic buildings; it is a vibrant educational experience that connects people with the past. It offers a unique opportunity to step back in time and understand the daily lives, challenges, and achievements of the Moravian settlers who helped shape North Carolina's history.

35. First Gold Rush: The nation's first gold rush started in 1799 when a 12-year-old found a 17-pound gold nugget in Cabarrus County.

36. Low-Cost Generic Drugs: The company Dr. Reddy's Laboratories in RTP has been pivotal in developing affordable generic medications.

37. Textile Innovations: High Point is known for innovations in textile machinery and furniture manufacturing techniques.

38. Solar Energy: North Carolina ranks second in the U.S. for solar energy production, pioneering green energy initiatives.

39. The North Carolina Symphony: A Legacy of Musical Excellence

The North Carolina Symphony, founded in 1932, holds a distinguished place in the cultural landscape of the state. As one of the first symphony orchestras supported by state funding, it has played a pivotal role in bringing classical music to the people of North Carolina. With its headquarters in Raleigh, the Symphony performs over 175 concerts annually, reaching diverse audiences across the state.

The Symphony's mission extends beyond entertainment; it is deeply committed to education and community engagement. Through its extensive outreach programs, the Symphony introduces classical music to thousands of schoolchildren each year. The annual Music

Discovery Program, for example, offers interactive sessions where young students can learn about different instruments and even participate in making music.

Over the decades, the North Carolina Symphony has collaborated with numerous world-renowned conductors and soloists, elevating its performances to international standards. Notable figures such as Leonard Bernstein, Yo-Yo Ma, and Itzhak Perlman have graced its stage, contributing to its reputation for artistic excellence. The Symphony's repertoire is diverse, ranging from classical masterpieces to contemporary works, ensuring that there is something for everyone to enjoy.

One of the Symphony's significant milestones was the opening of the Meymandi Concert Hall in 2001. This state-of-the-art venue, part of the Duke Energy Center for the Performing Arts in Raleigh, provides an acoustically superior space for performances, enhancing the audience's musical experience.

The North Carolina Symphony stands as a beacon of cultural enrichment, fostering a love for music in communities throughout the state. Its enduring presence and commitment to accessibility and education ensure that the joy of classical music can be enjoyed by all North Carolinians, regardless of their background or location.

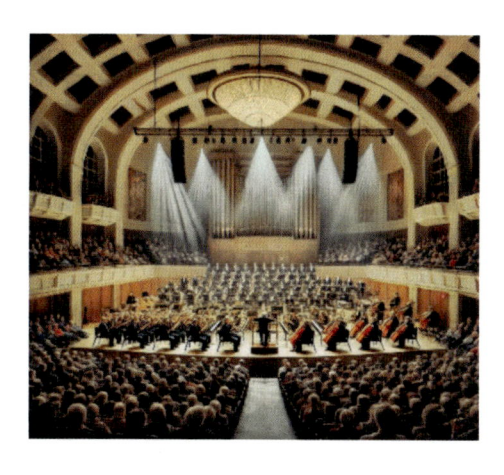

40. James Taylor: The iconic singer-songwriter spent much of his youth in Chapel Hill.

41. State Nickname: Known as the "Tar Heel State," referencing its history with naval stores like tar, pitch, and turpentine.

42. Great Dismal Swamp: Part of this vast swamp lies in North Carolina and is home to diverse wildlife and plants.

43. Ava Gardner: Hollywood's Timeless Star from North Carolina

Ava Gardner, born on December 24, 1922, in Grabtown, North Carolina, rose to become one of Hollywood's most iconic actresses. Her journey from a small tobacco farm to the glittering lights of Hollywood is a classic tale of talent and tenacity. Gardner's natural beauty and captivating presence caught the eye of MGM talent scouts when she was just a teenager, propelling her into the world of film.

Gardner's breakthrough role came in the 1946 film noir classic, "The Killers," where her performance as the alluring femme fatale Kitty Collins showcased her acting prowess. This role catapulted her to stardom and established her as a leading lady in Hollywood. Throughout her career, she starred in a variety of genres, from romantic dramas like "Mogambo" (1953) to epic historical films such as "The Barefoot Contessa" (1954).

Despite her success, Gardner remained deeply connected to her North Carolina roots. She often spoke fondly of her upbringing and the values instilled in her by her hardworking parents. Her legacy is preserved in the Ava Gardner Museum in Smithfield, North Carolina, which houses an extensive collection of her personal items, movie memorabilia, and costumes. The museum offers fans a glimpse into her life and career, celebrating her contributions to the film industry.

Gardner's influence extended beyond the silver screen. She was known for her spirited personality and her relationships with some of Hollywood's most famous men, including Frank Sinatra and Howard Hughes. Her enduring charm and talent have made her a timeless figure in the history of cinema, and her story continues to inspire aspiring actors from small towns to big cities.

44. Richard Petty: Known as "The King" of NASCAR, he is from Level Cross and won a record 200 races.

45. Uwharrie Mountains: One of the oldest mountain ranges in North America, located in central North Carolina.

46. Barbecue Tradition: The state is famous for its distinct styles of barbecue, particularly Eastern and Lexington styles.

47. Nina Simone: The High Priestess of Soul from North Carolina

Nina Simone, born Eunice Kathleen Waymon on February 21, 1933, in Tryon, North Carolina, was a musical prodigy who became a global icon. Simone's early life was steeped in music; she began playing the piano at the age of three and gave her first classical recital at twelve. Her immense talent earned her a scholarship to study at the prestigious Juilliard School in New York City.

Despite her classical training, Simone's career took a different path. She fused her classical prowess with jazz, blues, gospel, and soul, creating a unique and powerful sound that resonated with audiences worldwide. Her debut album, "Little Girl Blue" (1958), featured the hit "I Loves You, Porgy," which brought her international fame. Simone's music was deeply personal, often reflecting her experiences and the struggles of the African American community.

Simone was more than just a singer and pianist; she was a fervent advocate for civil rights. Her song "Mississippi Goddam," written in response to the 1963 bombing of the 16th Street Baptist Church in Birmingham, Alabama, became an anthem for the civil rights movement. She used her music to speak out against racial injustice and to inspire change, earning her the nickname "The High Priestess of Soul."

Throughout her career, Simone released over forty albums, each showcasing her versatility and emotional depth. Her powerful voice and intricate piano arrangements captivated audiences, leaving a lasting impact on the music industry. Despite facing numerous personal and professional challenges, including struggles with mental health and the pressures of fame, Simone's legacy endures.

Today, Nina Simone's contributions are celebrated worldwide. In Tryon, her childhood home has been preserved as a historic site, honoring her life and legacy. Simone's music continues to inspire new generations of artists, and her fearless spirit remains a symbol of resilience and resistance.

48. Zach Galifianakis: The comedian and actor, known for "The Hangover" series, hails from Wilkesboro.

49. Grandfather Mountain: Famous for its mile-high swinging bridge and breathtaking views.

50. Geographical Location: North Carolina is located in the southeastern region of the United States. It is bordered by several states and the Atlantic Ocean, giving it a diverse range of geographical features. To the north, North Carolina is bordered by Virginia, while to the south, it shares a border with South Carolina and Georgia. To the west lies Tennessee, and to the east, the state has a long coastline along the Atlantic Ocean.

The state's eastern coastline, known as the Outer Banks, is characterized by a string of narrow barrier islands and peninsulas that separate the Atlantic Ocean from the mainland. These islands are famous for their picturesque beaches, historic lighthouses, and wildlife refuges. Moving inland, the coastal plain stretches westward from the coastline and consists of low, flat land with rich, fertile soil, making it an ideal region for agriculture.

Further west, the Piedmont region is marked by rolling hills and is the state's most populous area, encompassing major cities such as

Raleigh, the state capital, Durham, and Charlotte, the largest city. This central region is known for its vibrant cultural and economic activities.

Continuing westward, the terrain becomes more rugged as it transitions into the Appalachian Mountains, which include the Great Smoky Mountains and the Blue Ridge Mountains. This mountainous region offers stunning landscapes, numerous outdoor recreational opportunities, and a cooler climate compared to the coastal and Piedmont areas.

North Carolina's diverse topography and climate zones contribute to its rich biodiversity and varied natural beauty, from sandy beaches to forested mountains, making it a state with a wide range of environmental and recreational attractions.

09

NORTH DAKOTA

1. Sitting Bull: The Legendary Lakota Leader

Sitting Bull, born around 1831 in what is now South Dakota, was a revered Hunkpapa Lakota chief and spiritual leader. He is best known for his role in resisting U.S. government policies aimed at confining his people to reservations. His leadership and vision for his people extended into North Dakota, where significant events in his life unfolded.

Sitting Bull was a fearless warrior from a young age, earning respect and leadership status within the Lakota Sioux. He became a prominent figure during the Sioux Wars of the late 19th century, leading his people in their struggle to maintain their lands and way of life. His most famous victory was at the Battle of Little Bighorn in 1876, where he, along with other Native American leaders, defeated General George Armstrong Custer and his troops.

After the victory, Sitting Bull and his followers fled to Canada to avoid retribution but returned to the United States in 1881 due to harsh conditions. They surrendered and were confined to the Standing Rock Reservation, which straddles North and South Dakota. During his time on the reservation, Sitting Bull continued to be a symbol of resistance and a spiritual leader for his people.

In 1885, he briefly toured with Buffalo Bill's Wild West Show, which provided a stark contrast to his life on the Plains but also offered him a platform to raise awareness about his people's plight. Despite his cooperation with the U.S. government, tensions remained high. In 1890, amid fears of the Ghost Dance movement, a spiritual revival among Native Americans, authorities attempted to arrest Sitting Bull. During the altercation, he was tragically killed.

Sitting Bull's legacy endures as a symbol of Native American resistance and resilience. His leadership and vision continue to inspire, and his life is commemorated in North Dakota, where visitors can learn about his contributions and the history of the Lakota people.

2. Theodore Roosevelt: The future U.S. president spent significant time in North Dakota and credited his experiences there with shaping his conservation policies.

3. Nonpartisan League: Founded in 1915 in North Dakota, it aimed to support farmers and promote progressive political reforms.

4. Dakota Territory: Before becoming a state, North Dakota was part of the Dakota Territory, which also included present-day South Dakota and parts of Montana and Wyoming.

5. The First Successful Heart-Lung Machine: A Medical Milestone

Dr. Dwight Emary Harken, a pioneering heart surgeon born in New England, North Dakota, is credited with the development and successful use of the first heart-lung machine. This groundbreaking device revolutionized the field of cardiac surgery and saved countless lives.

The heart-lung machine, also known as the cardiopulmonary bypass machine, takes over the functions of the heart and lungs during surgery, allowing surgeons to operate on a still and bloodless heart. Before its invention, heart surgery was extremely risky and limited in scope. The development of this machine marked a turning point in medical history, making complex cardiac surgeries feasible and dramatically improving patient outcomes.

Harken's work began during World War II, where he gained experience removing shrapnel from soldiers' hearts without stopping the heart. This experience laid the groundwork for his later innovations. After the war, he focused on developing a machine that could oxygenate and circulate blood outside the body, a concept that had been theorized but not successfully implemented.

In 1953, Dr. John Gibbon, building on the foundation laid by Harken and others, performed the first successful open-heart surgery using a heart-lung machine on an 18-year-old woman with a congenital heart defect. This landmark surgery demonstrated the machine's potential and opened the door to a new era of cardiac care.

North Dakota celebrates Dr. Harken's contributions to medical science. His work not only improved the lives of countless patients but also paved the way for ongoing advancements in cardiac surgery and critical care. The heart-lung machine remains a cornerstone of modern medicine, and its development is a testament to the innovative spirit and dedication of pioneers like Harken.

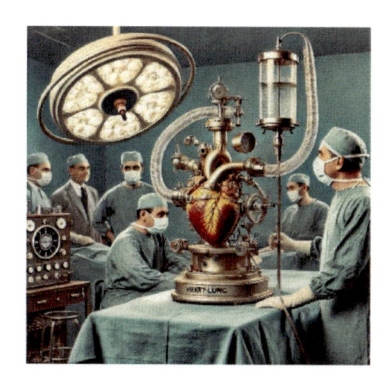

6. Statehood: North Dakota became the 39th state on November 2, 1889, the same day as South Dakota

7. Lewis and Clark Expedition: North Dakota was a significant part of the Lewis and Clark Expedition in 1804-1806. They spent their first winter at Fort Mandan, near present-day Washburn.

8. Fort Union: A major fur trading post on the Upper Missouri River, operational from 1828 to 1867.

9. Railroads: The completion of the Northern Pacific Railway in the 19th century was pivotal in North Dakota's settlement and economic development.

10. Prairie Potholes of North Dakota: Nature's Wetland Wonders

The Prairie Potholes of North Dakota are a unique and vital natural feature, formed thousands of years ago during the last Ice Age. As glaciers retreated, they left behind thousands of depressions across the landscape, creating a region now known as the Prairie Pothole Region. These potholes, or shallow wetlands, are essential to the state's ecosystem and play a crucial role in supporting wildlife, particularly migratory birds.

The Prairie Pothole Region spans parts of five states and three Canadian provinces, but North Dakota boasts one of the most extensive and dense collections of these wetlands. These small, shallow, water-filled depressions are scattered across the state's grasslands, providing critical habitats for a variety of plant and animal species. They range in size from less than an acre to several acres and can be temporary or permanent, depending on precipitation and groundwater levels.

One of the most significant roles of the prairie potholes is their function as a breeding ground for migratory waterfowl. North Dakota's potholes are often referred to as "America's Duck Factory" because they support more than half of North America's breeding duck population. Species such as mallards, teal, and pintails rely on these wetlands for nesting and raising their young.

Besides supporting bird populations, prairie potholes also contribute to flood control, groundwater recharge, and water purification. The wetlands act as natural sponges, absorbing excess rainwater and slowly releasing it, which helps mitigate flooding. They also filter out pollutants and sediments, improving water quality in the region.

Despite their ecological importance, prairie potholes face threats from agricultural expansion and climate change. Conservation efforts are crucial to protect these wetlands and the biodiversity they support. Programs like the Conservation Reserve Program (CRP) and partnerships with organizations such as Ducks Unlimited work to preserve and restore these vital habitats.

Visitors to North Dakota can explore the Prairie Pothole Region and witness the incredible diversity of wildlife it supports. The wetlands' serene beauty and ecological significance make them a natural treasure of the state.

11. Gold Rush: The Black Hills Gold Rush of the late 19th century brought many prospectors through North Dakota.

12. Great Plains: North Dakota is part of the Great Plains, characterized by vast, flat expanses of grassland.

13. Missouri River: This major river runs through the western part of the state, providing water and transportation routes.

14. Red River Valley: The Breadbasket of North Dakota

The Red River Valley, stretching along the eastern border of North Dakota and into Minnesota and Manitoba, is one of the most fertile agricultural regions in North America. This flat, expansive valley is named after the Red River of the North, which flows northward into Canada and eventually into Hudson Bay. The valley's rich, alluvial soil and favorable climate conditions make it ideal for farming, earning it the nickname "Breadbasket of the World."

The fertile soils of the Red River Valley were deposited by the ancient glacial Lake Agassiz, which covered the area thousands of years ago. As the lake receded, it left behind nutrient-rich sediments that now support a thriving agricultural industry. The region is known for producing high yields of crops such as wheat, barley, soybeans, corn, and sugar beets. The valley is particularly famous for its hard red spring wheat, which is highly valued for bread making.

The agricultural success of the Red River Valley has shaped the economic and cultural landscape of North Dakota. Small towns and communities throughout the valley are centered around farming activities, with many families having farmed the land for generations. The region's agricultural heritage is celebrated through various festivals and events, such as the Red River Valley Fair, which showcases local produce, livestock, and farming equipment.

The Red River Valley is also a site of historical significance. It was a key area for early European exploration and fur trading in the 18th and 19th centuries. The Hudson's Bay Company and the North West Company established trading posts along the Red River, facilitating trade with Indigenous peoples and helping to open the region to further settlement.

However, the Red River Valley is not without its challenges. The flat terrain and heavy clay soils can lead to significant flooding, particularly during spring thaw. The Red River is notorious for its periodic floods, which have caused extensive damage to communities over the years. Efforts to manage and mitigate flooding include levees, floodways, and diversion channels, as well as improved forecasting and emergency response systems.

Today, the Red River Valley remains a vital agricultural hub, contributing significantly to North Dakota's economy and food production. Its rich history, agricultural prominence, and natural beauty make it an essential part of the state's identity.

15. State Bank of North Dakota: Established in 1919, it is the only state-owned bank in the United States.

16. Theodore Roosevelt Rough Rider Award: Established in 1961, it honors North Dakotans who have achieved national recognition.

17. Custer Trail: The route taken by General Custer and his troops to the Little Bighorn passes through North Dakota.

18. Theodore Roosevelt's Ranch: The Elkhorn Ranch, where Roosevelt lived, is a historical site preserved within Theodore Roosevelt National Park.

19. Northwest Angle Dispute: A Geographic Quirk of North Dakota

The Northwest Angle, often simply referred to as "The Angle," is a unique geographic feature and a result of a historic boundary dispute between the United States and Great Britain. This small, isolated part of Minnesota is the only place in the contiguous United States that lies north of the 49th parallel, but its story is closely tied to North Dakota due to its geographic and historical context.

The dispute dates back to the Treaty of Paris in 1783, which ended the American Revolutionary War. The treaty's language regarding the boundary between the United States and British Canada was ambiguous and based on inaccurate maps. The key phrase mentioned the boundary running along a "line drawn from the most northwestern point of the Lake of the Woods" to the Mississippi River. However, explorers later discovered that the source of the Mississippi was south of the Lake of the Woods, leaving a small portion of land disconnected from the rest of the United States.

In 1818, the U.S. and Britain agreed to the 49th parallel as the border, but the Northwest Angle remained an anomaly. It created a geopolitical curiosity, with about 123 square miles of land only accessible by traveling through Canada or crossing the Lake of the Woods.

The Angle is part of Minnesota, but its unique location has created a sense of isolation and distinct community identity. It's home to about 120 residents and offers a remote, scenic landscape popular for fishing and outdoor activities.

Despite its isolation, the Northwest Angle has maintained strong ties to both the United States and Canada. Visitors often find it a fascinating place to explore, not just for its natural beauty but also for its quirky status as a geographic oddity resulting from a centuries-old boundary dispute.

20. First North Dakota Legislature: The first session was held in 1889, establishing the framework for the state's government.

21. University of North Dakota: Founded in 1883, it is the state's oldest and largest university, with a rich history of academic achievement.

22. International Peace Garden: Established in 1932, the garden on the U.S.-Canada border symbolizes peace and cooperation between the two countries.

23. North Dakota State Capitol Fire: The original state capitol building in Bismarck burned down in 1930 and was replaced by the current art deco building.

24. Carl Ben Eielson: North Dakota's Pioneering Aviator

Carl Ben Eielson, born on July 20, 1897, in Hatton, North Dakota, is celebrated as one of aviation's early pioneers. Eielson's contributions to the field of aviation are remarkable, particularly his achievements in Arctic exploration and air transport, which earned him international acclaim and numerous honors.

Eielson's passion for aviation was sparked during his service in World War I, where he trained as a pilot. After the war, he returned to North Dakota and pursued a career in aviation. His early efforts included barnstorming and establishing a flying school, but his ambitions soon led him to more challenging and groundbreaking endeavors.

In the 1920s, Eielson's career took a significant turn when he began working with polar explorer Hubert Wilkins. In 1928, they made history by completing the first successful trans-Arctic flight from Point Barrow, Alaska, to Spitsbergen, Norway. This daring journey covered over 2,200 miles of uncharted Arctic territory, showcasing the potential of aviation for exploration and transportation in the harshest environments.

Eielson's pioneering spirit didn't stop there. He became a key figure in the development of commercial air transport in Alaska, founding Alaskan Airways and making crucial contributions to the region's connectivity. His expertise in flying in extreme conditions made him an invaluable asset for rescue missions and delivering supplies to remote areas.

Tragically, Eielson's life was cut short in 1929 when he and his mechanic, Earl Borland, perished in a crash while attempting a rescue mission in Siberia. Despite his untimely death, Eielson's legacy endures. He is remembered as a fearless aviator who pushed the boundaries of what was possible in aviation.

North Dakota honors Carl Ben Eielson's legacy through various memorials, including the Eielson Air Force Base in Alaska, named in his honor. His life and achievements continue to inspire aviators and adventurers worldwide.

25. Highest Point: White Butte, at 3,506 feet, is the highest point in North Dakota.

26. The Homestead Act: Shaping North Dakota's Settlement

The Homestead Act of 1862 was a pivotal piece of legislation that significantly influenced the settlement and development of North Dakota. Signed into law by President Abraham Lincoln, the act aimed to encourage westward expansion by providing 160 acres of public land to any adult citizen or intended citizen who would improve the land by building a dwelling and cultivating crops for at least five years.

This act had a profound impact on North Dakota, drawing thousands of settlers to the region in search of new opportunities and a chance to own land. The fertile soil and promise of a fresh start attracted diverse groups of people, including European immigrants from Germany, Norway, Sweden, and Russia. These settlers played a crucial role in shaping the cultural and agricultural landscape of the state.

Homesteaders faced numerous challenges, including harsh weather conditions, isolation, and the arduous task of breaking the tough prairie sod to plant crops. Despite these difficulties, the promise of land ownership motivated many to persevere. Communities began to spring up, with settlers building homes, schools, churches, and businesses, laying the foundation for future growth and prosperity.

By the early 20th century, millions of acres in North Dakota had been claimed under the Homestead Act. The act not only facilitated the growth of the state's agricultural sector but also fostered a spirit of resilience and independence among its inhabitants. The legacy of the Homestead Act is still evident today in the strong agricultural traditions and tight-knit rural communities that characterize much of North Dakota.

The Homestead Act was eventually repealed in 1976, but its impact on North Dakota's development remains a significant chapter in the state's history. Visitors can explore historic homesteads and museums to gain a deeper understanding of the experiences of early settlers who transformed the vast prairies into thriving farmlands.

27. Women's Suffrage: North Dakota granted women the right to vote in school elections in 1883, ahead of the 19th Amendment.

28. Lake Sakakawea: This large reservoir, created by the Garrison Dam on the Missouri River, is a key water resource.

29. Coteau du Missouri: A prominent escarpment that divides the Missouri Plateau from the Drift Prairie.

30. Cloud Seeding in North Dakota: Weather Modification for Agriculture

Cloud seeding is an innovative weather modification technique that North Dakota has been utilizing since the 1950s to enhance precipitation and reduce hail damage. This scientific approach to weather control involves dispersing substances like silver iodide or sodium chloride into clouds to stimulate the formation of ice crystals, which can then grow and fall as rain or snow.

North Dakota's economy heavily relies on agriculture, making reliable rainfall crucial for crop production. The state experiences periodic droughts and severe thunderstorms that can threaten agricultural yields. To address these challenges, the North Dakota Cloud Modification Project (NDCMP) was established, aiming to increase rainfall during dry periods and minimize hail damage during storms.

The NDCMP operates in several counties, using aircraft equipped with cloud-seeding technology to target specific weather systems. Pilots release the seeding agents into the clouds, where they encourage the condensation process, leading to increased precipitation. This practice has shown positive results in boosting rainfall amounts and mitigating the impact of droughts on crops.

Additionally, cloud seeding helps reduce the size and frequency of hailstones, protecting valuable crops and reducing damage to property. Hail can be particularly devastating to farmers, causing significant financial losses. By promoting more rainfall and lessening hail damage, cloud seeding supports the agricultural economy and helps ensure food security.

While cloud seeding is not a guaranteed solution and its effectiveness can vary, it remains a valuable tool in North Dakota's arsenal for weather management. The state continues to invest in research and development to improve cloud seeding techniques and better understand its environmental impacts.

Visitors to North Dakota can learn about cloud seeding and its role in the state's agricultural success through educational exhibits and programs offered by the NDCMP and local museums. This innovative approach to weather modification exemplifies the state's commitment to supporting its farmers and adapting to the challenges posed by nature.

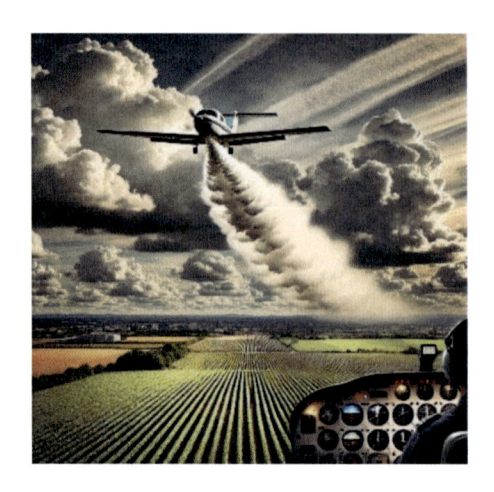

31. German-Russian Heritage: Many of North Dakota's early settlers were Germans from Russia, influencing the state's culture and cuisine.

32. Native American Tribes: The state is home to several tribes, including the Mandan, Hidatsa, Arikara, Lakota, and Dakota Sioux.

33. Scandinavian Heritage: Norwegian and Swedish immigrants have also left a significant cultural imprint on the state.

34. The First-Ever ATM for Horses: Innovation in North Dakota

In a unique blend of technology and tradition, North Dakota introduced the world's first ATM for horses. Located in the town of Medora, this innovative machine caters to horseback riders, allowing them to access cash without dismounting. This quirky invention highlights the state's deep connection to its western heritage and its embrace of modern conveniences.

The idea for the horse-friendly ATM emerged from the need to accommodate the numerous tourists and locals who explore

Medora and the surrounding areas on horseback. Medora is known for its rich history, cowboy culture, and the beautiful Theodore Roosevelt National Park. With many visitors choosing to experience the landscape on horseback, the ATM provides a practical solution for riders who need cash while out on the trails.

The ATM is specially designed to be accessible from horseback, with an elevated interface that riders can reach without getting off their horses. It features large, easy-to-read buttons and a secure enclosure to protect against weather conditions. The installation of this ATM has been met with enthusiasm, adding a touch of novelty to the town's charm and making life easier for horseback riders.

This innovation underscores North Dakota's blend of old and new, where traditional ways of life coexist with technological advancements. It also reflects the state's commitment to supporting tourism and enhancing the visitor experience in creative ways.

The horse-friendly ATM has garnered attention from media and visitors alike, becoming a unique attraction in Medora. It serves as a fun and functional reminder of North Dakota's western roots and its willingness to adapt to the needs of its community and visitors.

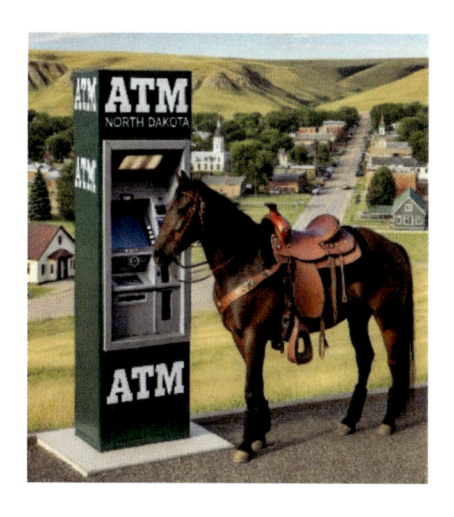

35. Air Quality: North Dakota consistently ranks high for air quality due to its low population density and regulatory measures.

36. Fossils: The Hell Creek Formation in North Dakota is rich in dinosaur fossils, including those of the Triceratops.

37. Wildlife Corridors: Projects are underway to establish and maintain wildlife corridors to ensure the safe movement of animals across the state.

38. Clint Hill: The Secret Service agent known for his role in protecting Jackie Kennedy during JFK's assassination was born in Larimore, North Dakota.

39. The First Operational Anti-Ballistic Missile Defense System: Stanley R. Mickelsen Safeguard Complex

The Stanley R. Mickelsen Safeguard Complex, located near Nekoma, North Dakota, holds the distinction of being the world's first operational anti-ballistic missile (ABM) defense system. Built during the height of the Cold War, this complex was part of the United States' efforts to protect against potential Soviet missile attacks.

Authorized by the Anti-Ballistic Missile Treaty of 1972, the complex was designed to detect and intercept incoming intercontinental ballistic missiles (ICBMs). Construction began in the early 1970s, and the facility became operational in October 1975. The complex featured a pyramid-shaped structure housing the Perimeter Acquisition Radar (PAR), which could detect and track multiple incoming missiles from thousands of miles away.

The heart of the system was the Sprint and Spartan missiles, which were designed to intercept and destroy enemy ICBMs. The Spartan missiles, equipped with nuclear warheads, were intended for long-range interception outside the Earth's atmosphere, while the Sprint missiles, with their incredible speed, were designed for short-range interception within the atmosphere. Together, these missiles provided a layered defense against potential nuclear attacks.

Despite its groundbreaking technology, the Stanley R. Mickelsen Safeguard Complex had a short operational life. Just one day after becoming fully operational, Congress voted to shut it down due to the high costs and changing defense strategies. By February 1976, the complex was deactivated, marking the end of its brief but significant role in missile defense history.

Today, the complex stands as a Cold War relic and a testament to the technological advancements and geopolitical tensions of the era. Its iconic pyramid structure remains a landmark, attracting visitors and history enthusiasts interested in the legacy of missile defense and the strategic importance of North Dakota during the Cold War.

40. First State-Owned Mill and Elevator: North Dakota established the first state-owned mill and elevator in the U.S., located in Grand Forks.

41. Home of Angie Dickinson: The legendary actress Angie Dickinson hails from Kulm, North Dakota.

42. Massive Sandhill Crane Migration: Every spring, thousands of sandhill cranes migrate through North Dakota, providing a spectacular wildlife viewing opportunity.

43. Pioneering Car Leasing: Donald Drake's Innovation

In the mid-20th century, North Dakota became the birthplace of a groundbreaking innovation that would forever change the automotive industry: car leasing. This innovative concept was pioneered by Donald Drake, a visionary entrepreneur from Fargo, North Dakota.

Drake's idea was simple yet revolutionary. He proposed a system where consumers could drive new cars without the long-term financial commitment of ownership. Instead of buying a vehicle outright, customers could lease it for a set period, typically two to three years, and then return it at the end of the lease term. This concept allowed individuals and businesses to enjoy the benefits of driving new vehicles while avoiding the burdens of depreciation and resale.

The first car leasing business, founded by Drake in the 1950s, faced initial skepticism. Many people were accustomed to the traditional model of car ownership and were wary of this new approach. However, Drake's persistence and innovative marketing strategies gradually won over customers. He highlighted the advantages of leasing, such as lower monthly payments, the ability to drive a new car every few years, and reduced maintenance costs.

Drake's pioneering efforts laid the foundation for the car leasing industry, which quickly gained traction across the United States.

By the 1960s, major automakers and financial institutions recognized the potential of leasing and began offering their own leasing programs. Today, car leasing is a mainstream option for consumers, accounting for a significant portion of new car transactions.

The impact of Donald Drake's innovation extends beyond the automotive industry. Car leasing has influenced consumer behavior, business operations, and even urban planning, as more people and companies opt for the flexibility and convenience it offers. North Dakota, particularly Fargo, can take pride in being the starting point of this transformative idea that continues to shape the automotive landscape.

44. Fire Hydrant Capital: The town of Grand Forks is known as the "Fire Hydrant Capital of the World" due to the many hydrants produced by its local manufacturers.

45. Simle Middle School's Humongous Hamburger: In 1999, Simle Middle School in Bismarck set a record by creating a 3,591-pound hamburger.

46. Famed Inventor Warren E. Burger: Chief Justice Warren E. Burger, known for his innovations in the judicial system, was born in Saint Paul, but his family moved to North Dakota where he spent much of his childhood.

47. Fargo: North Dakota's Largest City

Fargo, North Dakota's largest city, is a vibrant and dynamic hub of culture, education, and industry. Founded in 1871, Fargo began as a frontier town on the banks of the Red River and quickly grew into a bustling community due to its strategic location along the Northern Pacific Railway.

One of Fargo's defining features is its thriving arts and cultural scene. The city boasts numerous theaters, galleries, and music venues, reflecting a rich tapestry of creativity and expression. The Fargo Theatre, a historic Art Deco movie house built in 1926, is a centerpiece of downtown Fargo. It hosts the annual Fargo Film Festival, which attracts filmmakers and movie enthusiasts from around the world.

Education plays a significant role in Fargo's identity. North Dakota State University (NDSU), a major research institution, is located here and contributes to the city's youthful energy and innovation. NDSU's presence has fostered a strong entrepreneurial spirit, with many tech startups and businesses emerging from the university's research and development programs.

Fargo's economy is diverse, encompassing sectors such as technology, healthcare, manufacturing, and agriculture. The city is home to several major companies, including Microsoft, which has a large campus here. Fargo's robust economy and quality of life have earned it a reputation as one of the best places to live and work in the United States.

Fargo also embraces its history and heritage. The Plains Art Museum, located in a renovated warehouse, showcases contemporary and Native American art, celebrating the region's cultural roots. The annual Fargo Marathon and Fargo AirSho are popular events that draw participants and spectators from across the country.

Despite its growth and modernization, Fargo retains a strong sense of community and Midwestern friendliness. Its blend of historic charm and forward-thinking innovation makes Fargo a unique and appealing destination in North Dakota.

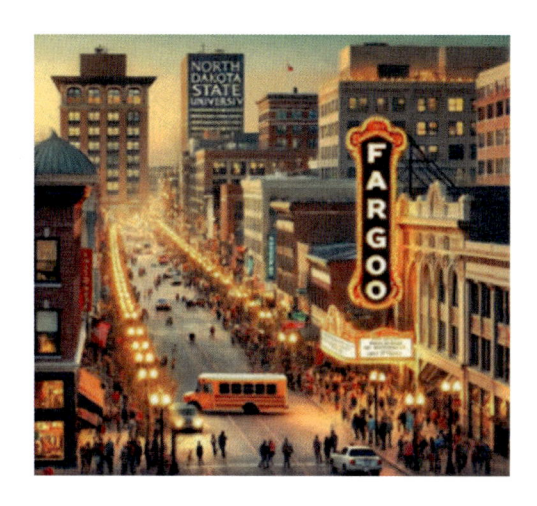

48. Bobcat Company: The skid-steer loader, a compact construction vehicle, was invented by the Bobcat Company, headquartered in West Fargo.

49. Bonanza Farms: In the late 19th century, North Dakota was known for its large-scale wheat farms, known as Bonanza farms, which were highly productive.

50. Geographical Location: North Dakota is located in the north-central region of the United States, within the Great Plains. It is bordered by several states and one Canadian province, giving it a unique geographical positioning. To the north, it shares an international boundary with the Canadian province of Manitoba, while to the west, it is bordered by Montana. South Dakota lies to the south, and Minnesota forms its eastern border.

The state's landscape is characterized by three distinct regions: the Red River Valley, the Drift Prairie, and the Missouri Plateau. The eastern part of North Dakota, known as the Red River Valley, is a flat, fertile plain formed by the ancient glacial Lake Agassiz.

This area is one of the most productive agricultural regions in the United States.

Moving westward, the Drift Prairie, also known as the Central Lowlands, features rolling hills and numerous small lakes. This region transitions into the Missouri Plateau, which covers the western part of the state. The Missouri Plateau includes the Badlands, a rugged area with unique rock formations and sparse vegetation, as well as the state's highest point, White Butte.

The Missouri River, one of North Dakota's significant waterways, flows from west to east through the central part of the state, providing essential water resources and recreation opportunities. The Souris and James Rivers are also notable watercourses that contribute to the state's hydrology.

North Dakota's climate varies from semi-arid in the west to humid continental in the east, with cold winters and warm summers. This climatic diversity supports a range of agricultural activities and contributes to the state's rich biodiversity.

Overall, North Dakota's geographical location and varied landscapes play a crucial role in its economy, culture, and natural environment, making it a distinctive part of the United States.

10

OHIO

1. The Cuyahoga River Fire: Catalyst for Environmental Reform

In 1969, the Cuyahoga River in Cleveland, Ohio, caught fire due to extensive pollution from industrial waste. This was not the first time the river had ignited, but it became the most famous incident, drawing national attention to the severe environmental degradation occurring in America's waterways. The fire lasted just 30 minutes, but the image of a river aflame symbolized the urgent need for environmental reform.

The Cuyahoga River Fire sparked a movement that led to significant legislative changes. In 1970, the Environmental Protection Agency (EPA) was established, and in 1972, the Clean Water Act was passed, both directly influenced by the public outcry following the fire. These measures aimed to reduce pollution and protect natural resources, setting the stage for modern environmental policy.

Today, the Cuyahoga River has undergone a remarkable transformation. Extensive cleanup efforts have restored the river's health, and it is now home to diverse wildlife and recreational activities. The river's resurgence is a testament to the power of environmental activism and effective regulation.

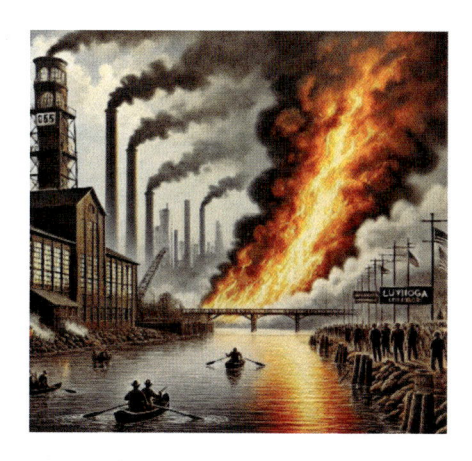

2. Statehood: Ohio became the 17th state in the Union on March 1, 1803.

3. Cleveland: Founded in 1796, Cleveland quickly became a major manufacturing and industrial center.

4. Civil War Contributions: Ohio provided more soldiers per capita to the Union Army than any other state.

5. Shaker Heights: A Model of Urban Planning

Shaker Heights, Ohio, founded in 1912 by the Van Sweringen brothers, is a testament to thoughtful urban planning and a commitment to community values. This Cleveland suburb was named after the Shakers, a religious sect known for their simple living and high-quality craftsmanship. The Van Sweringen brothers drew inspiration from the Shakers' principles to create a meticulously planned community that emphasized green spaces, cohesive architectural design, and efficient transportation.

The layout of Shaker Heights features wide, tree-lined streets, elegant Tudor-style homes, and ample public parks. The community was designed to be a suburban oasis, providing residents with a peaceful environment away from the hustle and bustle of urban life. The Van Sweringens also developed the Shaker Heights Rapid Transit, a light rail system that connected the suburb to downtown Cleveland, making commuting convenient for residents.

Beyond its physical beauty, Shaker Heights has been a leader in educational integration and diversity. In the 1950s and 60s, as racial tensions were high across the United States, Shaker Heights proactively implemented policies to promote integration in its schools. The community embraced voluntary desegregation efforts, ensuring that students of all races had equal access to quality education. This forward-thinking approach fostered a sense of inclusivity and set a national example for other communities.

Today, Shaker Heights continues to be celebrated for its historical architecture, cultural diversity, and strong community spirit. It is home to excellent schools, vibrant arts and cultural events, and active neighborhood associations. The city's commitment to preserving its heritage while embracing progress makes it a unique and appealing place to live.

6. Battle of Fallen Timbers: This 1794 battle near present-day Maumee was a decisive victory for the U.S. Army against Native American forces, leading to the Treaty of Greenville.

7. Marietta: Established in 1788, it was the first permanent settlement in the Northwest Territory.

8. Ohio Statehouse: Located in Columbus, it has been the seat of Ohio government since 1857 and features a distinctive Greek Revival architecture.

9. Toledo War: A boundary dispute between Ohio and Michigan in the 1830s, which ended peacefully with Ohio gaining the Toledo Strip.

10. Chillicothe: Ohio's First Capital and Historical Treasure

Chillicothe, established in 1796, is a city steeped in historical significance. Nestled along the banks of the Scioto River, it was the first and third capital of Ohio, playing a central role in the state's early development. Chillicothe served as the capital from 1803 to 1810 and again from 1812 to 1816 before the capital was permanently moved to Columbus.

As Ohio's first state capital, Chillicothe was the site of the state's first constitutional convention in 1802. During this convention, leaders drafted Ohio's first constitution, laying the groundwork for the state's government and legal system. This foundational document guided Ohio through its formative years and helped shape its identity.

Chillicothe is also known for its rich Native American heritage, particularly the ancient earthworks created by the Hopewell culture. These impressive mounds, some of which are preserved at the Hopewell Culture National Historical Park, offer valuable insights into the region's prehistoric past. The park attracts archaeologists, historians, and visitors interested in learning about the sophisticated societies that once thrived in the area.

The city's historical significance extends to the 19th century, with landmarks like the Adena Mansion and Gardens. This historic site was the home of Thomas Worthington, one of Ohio's early governors and a prominent political figure. The mansion and its beautifully landscaped gardens provide a glimpse into early 19th-century life and Worthington's contributions to Ohio's statehood.

Chillicothe's vibrant arts scene, historical architecture, and commitment to preserving its heritage make it a unique destination for history enthusiasts and visitors alike. The city's blend of historical charm and modern amenities ensures that it remains a vital part of Ohio's cultural landscape.

11. Cincinnati: Founded in 1788, it became a major trading and industrial hub due to its location on the Ohio River.

12. Akron: Known as the "Rubber Capital of the World," it was home to major rubber companies like Goodyear and Firestone.

13. Dayton Aviation Heritage National Historical Park: Celebrates the contributions of the Wright brothers and Paul Laurence Dunbar to aviation and literature, respectively.

14. John Rankin House: A Beacon of Freedom

The John Rankin House, located in Ripley, Ohio, stands as a symbol of hope and freedom in American history. Built in 1825, it was the home of Reverend John Rankin, a fervent abolitionist and conductor on the Underground Railroad. The house's strategic location on a hill overlooking the Ohio River made it an ideal sanctuary for escaping slaves seeking freedom in the North.

Reverend Rankin and his family were deeply committed to the abolitionist cause. They provided shelter, food, and guidance to hundreds of fugitive slaves. Rankin's home featured a lantern in the window, serving as a beacon to those crossing the river from the slave state of Kentucky. The Rankin House became one of the most active and well-known stations on the Underground Railroad.

Rankin's efforts were part of a broader network of abolitionists in Ohio who risked their lives to fight slavery. His passionate sermons and writings further galvanized anti-slavery sentiment in the region. The stories of courage and resilience associated with the Rankin House highlight the significant role Ohio played in the abolitionist movement.

Today, the John Rankin House is a National Historic Landmark, open to the public for tours and educational programs. Visitors can explore the home and learn about the Rankin family's extraordinary contributions to the fight for freedom. The house stands as a powerful reminder of the impact individuals can have in the pursuit of justice and equality.

15. Procter & Gamble: Founded in Cincinnati in 1837, it is one of the world's largest consumer goods companies.

16. Sherman House Museum: The birthplace of Civil War General William Tecumseh Sherman, located in Lancaster.

17. Zoar Village: Founded in 1817 by German Separatists, it is a well-preserved example of a 19th-century communal society.

18. Harriet Beecher Stowe House: The Cincinnati home of the author of "Uncle Tom's Cabin," which had a significant impact on anti-slavery sentiment.

19. The First Traffic Light: A Cleveland Innovation

The world's first electric traffic light was installed in Cleveland, Ohio, on August 5, 1914. Designed by James Hoge, this pioneering device was placed at the intersection of Euclid Avenue and East 105th Street. The traffic light featured red and green lights and a buzzer to signal color changes, significantly improving traffic control and safety in the bustling city.

Hoge's invention addressed the growing problem of traffic congestion and accidents in urban areas. The initial traffic light system was simple yet effective, with a manually operated switch to control the lights. The success of this initial installation led to widespread adoption in cities across the United States and around the world, revolutionizing traffic management.

Cleveland's role in this innovation highlights the city's historical significance in technological advancements. The original traffic light installation marked the beginning of modern traffic control systems, which continue to evolve with advancements in technology.

Today, traffic lights are an integral part of daily life, ensuring the safe and orderly flow of vehicles and pedestrians. The legacy of Cleveland's first traffic light is a testament to the city's contributions to urban infrastructure and innovation. The location of the original traffic light installation is commemorated with a plaque, celebrating this significant milestone in traffic management history.

20. Great Flood of 1913: Devastated much of Ohio, particularly the city of Dayton, leading to significant changes in flood control measures.

21. Ohio and Erie Canal: Completed in 1832, it connected Lake Erie to the Ohio River, boosting commerce and settlement.

22. Mound Builders: Prehistoric indigenous cultures like the Adena and Hopewell left behind significant earthworks, such as those at the Newark Earthworks.

23. Taft Museum of Art: Located in Cincinnati, it was the home of President William Howard Taft's half-brother and is now a prominent art museum.

24. Seven U.S. Presidents Born in Ohio: The Buckeye Legacy

Ohio is often called the "Mother of Presidents" because it is the birthplace of seven U.S. Presidents, the second-most of any state after Virginia. These presidents, born in the 19th century, played significant roles in shaping the nation's history. Their contributions to the country reflect Ohio's rich political heritage.

1. **Ulysses S. Grant** (1822-1885): Born in Point Pleasant, Grant was the commanding general who led the Union Army to victory during the Civil War and served two terms as the 18th President. His presidency focused on Reconstruction and civil rights for freed slaves.

2. **Rutherford B. Hayes** (1822-1893): Born in Delaware, Hayes became the 19th President after a highly contested election. His presidency is known for ending Reconstruction and restoring local control to Southern states.

3. **James A. Garfield** (1831-1881): Born in Moreland Hills, Garfield served as the 20th President. His term was cut short by assassination, but he is remembered for his advocacy of civil service reform.

4. **Benjamin Harrison** (1833-1901): Born in North Bend, Harrison was the 23rd President and the grandson of William Henry Harrison, the 9th President. His administration is noted for economic legislation, including the McKinley Tariff and the Sherman Antitrust Act.

5. **William McKinley** (1843-1901): Born in Niles, McKinley served as the 25th President. His presidency is remembered for leading the nation to victory in the Spanish-American War and promoting economic growth through protective tariffs.

6. **William Howard Taft** (1857-1930): Born in Cincinnati, Taft was the 27th President and later the 10th Chief Justice of the United States, making him the only person to have held both offices. His presidency focused on trust-busting and civil service reform.

7. **Warren G. Harding** (1865-1923): Born in Blooming Grove, Harding served as the 29th President. His administration is

often remembered for scandals, but he also promoted peace and economic growth following World War I.

These presidents collectively shaped the political landscape of the United States during critical periods of its history. Their Ohio roots underscore the state's significant influence on national politics. Visitors can explore various historical sites and museums dedicated to these leaders, gaining insights into their lives and legacies.

25. Ohio State Reformatory: This historic prison in Mansfield is known for its architecture and for being a filming location for "The Shawshank Redemption."

26. Cleveland Clinic: A Global Leader in Healthcare

Founded in 1921, the Cleveland Clinic is one of the most prestigious medical centers in the world, renowned for its cutting-edge research, patient care, and medical education. Located in Cleveland, Ohio, this nonprofit, multispecialty academic medical center was established by four physicians—George Washington Crile, Frank E. Bunts, William E. Lower, and John Phillips—with the vision of providing outstanding patient care combined with research and education.

The Cleveland Clinic has consistently ranked among the top hospitals in the United States, particularly noted for its cardiology and heart surgery programs. The Clinic's Heart and Vascular Institute has been ranked number one in the nation for over two decades, pioneering numerous advances in cardiovascular medicine, including minimally invasive heart surgeries and innovative treatments for heart disease.

In addition to cardiology, the Cleveland Clinic excels in a wide range of medical specialties, including neurology, gastroenterology, and cancer treatment. The institution is also a leader in medical research, with numerous clinical trials and studies contributing to the advancement of medical science. Its Lerner Research Institute is one of the largest research institutes in the country, focusing on basic, translational, and clinical research.

The Cleveland Clinic's commitment to education is evident in its Lerner College of Medicine, which offers a unique curriculum designed to train future physician-scientists. The Clinic also provides extensive residency and fellowship programs across various specialties, ensuring that the next generation of healthcare providers is well-prepared.

The Cleveland Clinic's innovative approach and dedication to patient care, research, and education have solidified its position as a global leader in healthcare. Its ongoing contributions to medical science continue to improve patient outcomes and shape the future of medicine.

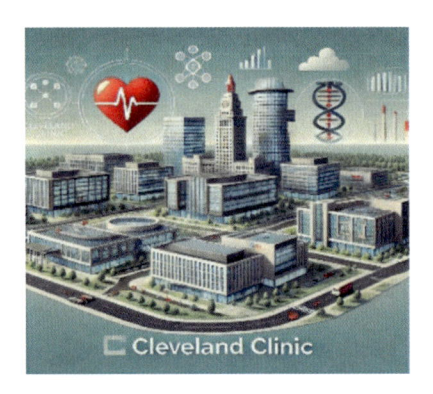

27. David Grohl Alley: In Warren, Ohio, there is an alley named after the Foo Fighters' lead singer and former Nirvana drummer, David Grohl, who was born there.

28. Quaker Oats: The Quaker Oats Company was founded in Ravenna, Ohio, and became a household name for its breakfast cereals.

29. First Ambulance Service: The first ambulance service in the U.S. was established in Cincinnati in 1865.

30. Spring Grove Cemetery: A Historic Garden Cemetery

Established in 1845 in Cincinnati, Ohio, Spring Grove Cemetery is one of the largest and most beautiful garden cemeteries in the United States. Designed by renowned landscape architect Adolph Strauch, Spring Grove spans 733 acres and is known for its serene landscapes, historic monuments, and botanical diversity.

Spring Grove Cemetery was created during a period when the rural cemetery movement was gaining popularity in the United States. These cemeteries were designed to be more than just burial grounds; they were intended as public parks that provided a tranquil environment for reflection and recreation. Spring Grove exemplifies this concept with its winding paths, picturesque lakes, and meticulously maintained gardens.

The cemetery is the final resting place for many notable figures, including Civil War generals, prominent politicians, and influential business leaders. One of the most famous individuals buried here is Salmon P. Chase, a former Chief Justice of the United States and Secretary of the Treasury under President Abraham Lincoln. The cemetery's rich history is reflected in its diverse array of monuments and mausoleums, which range from simple headstones to elaborate Victorian structures.

Spring Grove is also a certified arboretum, home to an impressive collection of trees and plants. The cemetery's horticultural staff takes great care in preserving and enhancing the landscape, ensuring that it remains a living, evolving work of art. Visitors can explore the grounds and enjoy the beauty of blooming flowers, majestic trees, and peaceful water features.

In addition to its historical and botanical significance, Spring Grove Cemetery hosts various community events, including guided tours, educational programs, and seasonal activities. These events offer visitors the opportunity to learn about the cemetery's history, architecture, and natural beauty while fostering a sense of community.

Spring Grove Cemetery remains a cherished landmark in Cincinnati, celebrated for its historical importance, stunning landscapes, and commitment to preserving both history and nature.

31. Wendy's: The fast-food chain was founded by Dave Thomas in Columbus, Ohio, in 1969.

32. Antarctic Discoverer: Admiral Richard E. Byrd, an American naval officer who led expeditions to Antarctica, was born in Winchester, Ohio.

33. Mike Tyson: The former heavyweight boxing champion was born in Cleveland, Ohio.

34. Gnadenhutten Massacre: A Tragic Chapter in Ohio's History

The Gnadenhutten Massacre is one of the darkest episodes in Ohio's history, illustrating the tragic consequences of frontier conflicts during the American Revolutionary War. On March 8, 1782, in the village of Gnadenhutten, located in present-day eastern Ohio, 96 Christian Delaware (Lenape) Native Americans—mostly women and children—were brutally murdered by Pennsylvania militiamen.

The village of Gnadenhutten, meaning "Tents of Grace," was established in 1772 by Moravian missionaries who sought to convert the Delaware people to Christianity. The Moravians and their converts adopted a pacifist lifestyle, focusing on farming and religious worship. Despite their neutrality in the ongoing conflict between American settlers and Native American tribes allied with the British, the inhabitants of Gnadenhutten were not spared from suspicion and violence.

In early 1782, a group of Pennsylvania militiamen, seeking retribution for recent Native American attacks on frontier settlements, targeted Gnadenhutten. Mistakenly believing that the peaceful Christian Delaware were involved in these attacks, the militiamen lured them into the village and disarmed them under the pretense of relocating them to Fort Pitt for their safety. Once disarmed, the militiamen accused the villagers of participating in raids and sentenced them to death.

The massacre was carried out methodically, with the victims imprisoned in two separate buildings and then brutally killed with mallets and hatchets. The massacre left an indelible mark on the region and fueled ongoing hostilities between Native Americans and American settlers.

Today, the Gnadenhutten Massacre is commemorated at the Gnadenhutten Museum and Monument. The site includes a reconstructed mission house, a burial mound containing the remains of the victims, and a museum that tells the story of the massacre and the broader context of Native American and colonial interactions in the region. The site serves as a somber reminder of the past and a call to remember the consequences of intolerance and violence.

35. Pro Football Hall of Fame: Located in Canton, it honors the greatest players, coaches, and contributors to the sport of professional football.

36. Neil Armstrong: The first man to walk on the moon was born in Wapakoneta, Ohio.

37. Rock and Roll Hall of Fame: Located in Cleveland, it celebrates the history and influence of rock music and its artists.

38. Cedar Point: Known as the "Roller Coaster Capital of the World," Cedar Point in Sandusky has some of the tallest and fastest roller coasters.

39. Fort Meigs: A Stronghold in the War of 1812

Fort Meigs, located in present-day Perrysburg, Ohio, played a crucial role in the War of 1812, serving as a key stronghold for American forces in the Northwest Territory. Constructed in early 1813 under the command of General William Henry Harrison, Fort Meigs was strategically positioned on the south bank of the Maumee River to protect the Ohio frontier from British and Native American attacks.

The fort's construction was a direct response to the British capture of Detroit and their subsequent control over much of the Great Lakes region. General Harrison, recognizing the strategic importance of controlling the Maumee River and preventing further British incursions into Ohio, ordered the building of Fort Meigs. The fort was named in honor of Ohio Governor Return J. Meigs Jr.

Fort Meigs faced its first major test in May 1813, during the First Siege of Fort Meigs. British forces, allied with Native American warriors led by Tecumseh, laid siege to the fort. Despite intense bombardment and several assaults, the fort's defenders, bolstered by reinforcements from Kentucky, successfully repelled the attackers. This victory boosted American morale and hindered British plans to advance further into the Northwest Territory.

A second siege occurred in July 1813, but the attackers were once again unsuccessful in capturing the fort. The resilience and strategic importance of Fort Meigs helped secure American control over the region and contributed to the eventual American victory in the War of 1812.

Today, Fort Meigs is a well-preserved historic site and museum. Visitors can explore the reconstructed fort, including its blockhouses, artillery batteries, and defensive earthworks. The site offers educational programs, reenactments, and exhibits that provide insight into the fort's role in the War of 1812 and the broader conflict between the United States, Britain, and Native American nations.

40. NASA Glenn Research Center: Located in Cleveland, this center is a key site for aeronautics and space research.

41. Buckeye Candy: A popular confection in Ohio, resembling the buckeye nut, consists of peanut butter dipped in chocolate.

42. Toni Morrison: The Nobel Prize-winning author of "Beloved" and other works was born in Lorain, Ohio.

43. The Discovery of Teflon: A Serendipitous Breakthrough

The discovery of Teflon, a non-stick and heat-resistant material, was a serendipitous event that revolutionized numerous industries. In 1938, chemist Roy Plunkett, who was working for DuPont in Deepwater, New Jersey, made this accidental discovery. Plunkett, originally from Ohio, was researching new refrigerants when he stumbled upon polytetrafluoroethylene (PTFE), which would later be branded as Teflon.

Plunkett was experimenting with tetrafluoroethylene gas, attempting to develop a new type of refrigerant. He stored the gas in small cylinders at low temperatures. One day, when he opened a cylinder, he found that the gas had disappeared. Instead, he discovered a strange, white, waxy substance lining the inside of the cylinder. Intrigued, Plunkett and his team conducted further tests and realized that the substance had remarkable properties: it was extremely slippery, non-reactive, and had a high melting point.

Recognizing the potential applications of this new material, DuPont patented PTFE in 1941 and registered the Teflon trademark in 1945. Initially, Teflon was used in military and industrial applications during World War II, including coating valves and seals in the Manhattan Project. Its non-reactive nature made it ideal for use in corrosive environments.

Teflon's most famous application came in the 1960s when it was introduced to the consumer market as a non-stick coating for cookware. This innovation transformed cooking and cleaning, making Teflon-coated pans a staple in kitchens worldwide. Beyond cookware, Teflon is now used in a wide range of products, including electrical insulation, aerospace technology, and medical devices.

The discovery of Teflon is a prime example of how accidental scientific discoveries can lead to groundbreaking advancements. Roy Plunkett's curiosity and perseverance turned an unexpected finding into a material that continues to have a profound impact on modern life.

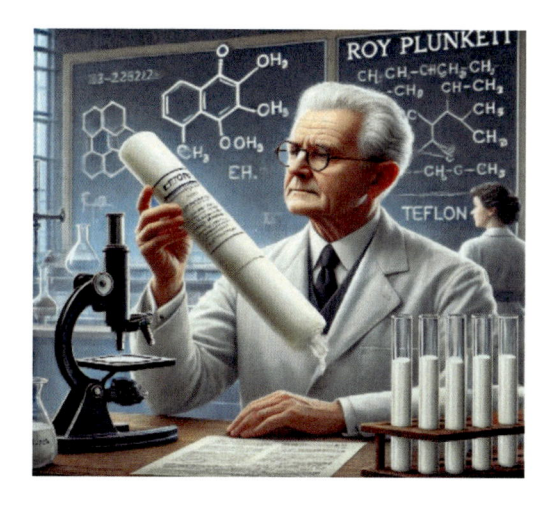

44. Superman: The iconic superhero Superman was created by Jerry Siegel and Joe Shuster while they were living in Cleveland.

45. Battle of Lake Erie: Fought in 1813, it was a pivotal naval engagement in the War of 1812, ensuring American control of the lake.

46. The Wilds: Located on reclaimed coal mine land, it is one of the largest wildlife conservation centers in North America.

47. The First Cash Register: Securing Honest Transactions

The invention of the cash register was a pivotal moment in retail history, greatly enhancing the security and efficiency of financial transactions. This groundbreaking device was invented by James Ritty, a saloon owner from Dayton, Ohio, in 1879. Ritty's invention was driven by his frustration with employees stealing money from his establishment.

Ritty observed that dishonest employees could easily pocket cash from sales without leaving any record of the transaction. Determined to find a solution, he designed a machine that would keep an accurate count of sales and secure the money. He called his invention the "Incorruptible Cashier."

The first cash register was a mechanical marvel. It featured a series of keys, each representing a different amount of money. When a key was pressed, it would register the sale by advancing a dial that displayed the total amount of the transaction. The machine also produced a distinct bell sound, signaling that a sale had been recorded. This feature provided an auditory confirmation of each transaction, deterring theft and ensuring transparency.

Ritty's invention quickly gained popularity among business owners who faced similar challenges with employee theft. In 1884, Ritty sold his patent to John H. Patterson, who recognized the device's potential and founded the National Cash Register Company (NCR) in Dayton. Under Patterson's leadership, NCR improved and mass-produced the cash register, incorporating additional features such as receipts and customer displays.

The cash register revolutionized the retail industry by providing a reliable and secure method for recording sales. It helped businesses maintain accurate financial records, reduce losses due to theft, and improve customer trust. The success of the cash register also laid the foundation for further advancements in retail technology, including the development of modern point-of-sale systems.

Today, the cash register remains an iconic symbol of retail innovation, representing the enduring impact of James Ritty's ingenuity.

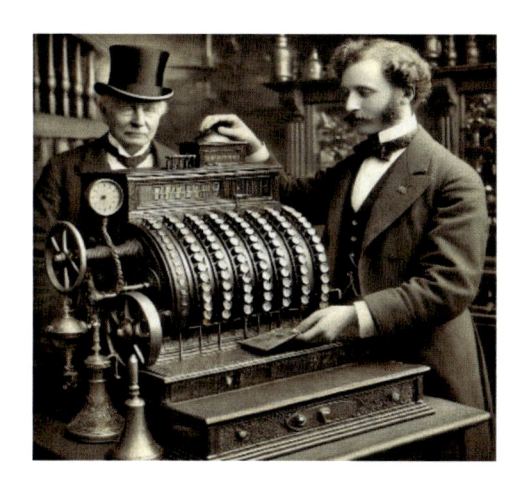

48. Thomas Edison Birthplace: Located in Milan, it commemorates the life of the famous inventor who was born there in 1847.

49. National Museum of the U.S. Air Force: Located near Dayton, it is the oldest and largest military aviation museum in the world.

50. Geographical Location: Ohio is located in the Midwestern region of the United States, bordered by several states and a Great Lake. To the north, Ohio shares a border with Michigan and has a shoreline along Lake Erie, one of the five Great Lakes, which provides access to major shipping routes and recreational opportunities. To the east, Ohio is bordered by Pennsylvania, and to the southeast, it touches West Virginia along the Ohio River, a significant waterway for transportation and commerce.

To the south, Ohio is bordered by Kentucky, with the Ohio River continuing to form a natural boundary. This river is historically and economically significant, providing a route for trade and travel. To the west, Ohio shares a border with Indiana. The state's central location within the Midwest makes it a crucial link between the Eastern states and the rest of the country.

Ohio's landscape is diverse, featuring flat plains in the west, rolling hills in the central region, and the Appalachian Plateau in the southeast. This varied topography contributes to the state's agricultural productivity, with fertile soils supporting crops like corn, soybeans, and wheat.

The state's major rivers, including the Ohio River, the Cuyahoga River, and the Scioto River, play important roles in its geography and economy. Ohio's capital, Columbus, is centrally located and serves as a major transportation and logistics hub, benefiting from the state's extensive network of highways and railroads.

Ohio's climate is generally humid continental, with hot summers and cold winters, though it varies slightly across the state due to its diverse geography. This climate supports a wide range of outdoor activities and contributes to the state's rich biodiversity.

Overall, Ohio's strategic location in the heart of the Midwest, its access to major waterways, and its diverse landscape make it a significant state both geographically and economically within the United States.

11

OKLAHOMA

1. The Trail of Tears in Oklahoma:

The Trail of Tears is a profoundly tragic chapter in American history, particularly significant to Oklahoma. In the 1830s, the United States government forcibly removed thousands of Native Americans from their ancestral homelands in the southeastern United States. This forced migration is known as the Trail of Tears, a journey marked by immense suffering and loss.

The Indian Removal Act of 1830, signed by President Andrew Jackson, set the stage for this mass relocation. The Cherokee, along with other tribes like the Choctaw, Chickasaw, Creek, and Seminole, were compelled to leave their lands. The government promised them new territories west of the Mississippi River, in present-day Oklahoma, which was designated as Indian Territory.

The journey to Oklahoma was harrowing. Native Americans traveled by foot, horse, wagon, and even boat, under dire conditions. They faced disease, harsh weather, and inadequate supplies. An estimated 4,000 Cherokee people died from hunger, exposure, and disease. The term "Trail of Tears" reflects the immense grief and suffering endured during this forced exodus.

Upon reaching Oklahoma, the Native American tribes worked to rebuild their communities and preserve their cultures. Despite the immense hardships, they demonstrated remarkable resilience. Today, Oklahoma is home to many Native American tribes who continue to honor their heritage and remember the Trail of Tears as a crucial part of their history.

The Trail of Tears is a somber reminder of the injustices faced by Native Americans and their enduring spirit. It serves as a crucial lesson about the importance of respecting and protecting the rights and lands of indigenous peoples.

2. Statehood: Oklahoma became the 46th state on November 16, 1907.

3. Indian Territory: Before statehood, much of Oklahoma was designated as Indian Territory, a region set aside for Native American tribes.

4. Dust Bowl: During the 1930s, Oklahoma was severely affected by the Dust Bowl, causing mass migration and significant economic hardship.

5. The Land Run of 1889:

The Land Run of 1889 was a significant event in Oklahoma's history that dramatically shaped the state's development. On April 22, 1889, thousands of settlers raced to claim land in what was then known as the Unassigned Lands, which later became part of Oklahoma Territory.

The origins of the Land Run lie in the government's decision to open up these lands to non-Native American settlers. These lands had previously been designated for Native American tribes following their forced relocation, but over time, some areas were declared surplus and made available for settlement.

At precisely noon on April 22, a gunshot signaled the start of the land rush. Thousands of hopeful settlers, known as "Boomers," surged into the territory by horse, wagon, bicycle, and even on foot, all vying to stake their claim. The scene was chaotic and exhilarating, with people racing to secure a plot of land that they could call their own.

The Land Run led to the rapid establishment of new towns and communities. Cities like Oklahoma City and Guthrie sprang up almost overnight. The process of claiming land was governed by strict rules, and settlers had to follow specific procedures to secure their claims. Despite these regulations, the land rush was marked by disputes and conflicts as people raced to grab the best plots.

The Land Run of 1889 is a testament to the adventurous and entrepreneurial spirit of the settlers. It also marked a significant shift in the region's demographics and laid the foundation for Oklahoma's growth and development. Today, the Land Run is remembered as a pivotal moment in the state's history, reflecting both the opportunities and challenges of the frontier era.

6. First Capital: The original capital of Oklahoma was Guthrie before it was moved to Oklahoma City in 1910.

7. Oil Boom: Oklahoma experienced an oil boom in the early 20th century, which led to rapid economic growth and development.

8. Cattle Drives: Oklahoma was a major route for cattle drives in the 19th century, contributing to its cowboy culture.

9. Route 66: The iconic Route 66 runs through Oklahoma, playing a significant role in the state's transportation history.

10. Black Wall Street in Tulsa, Oklahoma:

Black Wall Street, located in the Greenwood District of Tulsa, Oklahoma, was one of the most prosperous African American communities in the United States in the early 20th century. Established in the early 1900s, it became a hub of African American entrepreneurship and culture, often referred to as "a Black Wall Street" due to its significant economic success.

The district was home to numerous black-owned businesses, including banks, hotels, cafes, movie theaters, and luxury shops. One notable figure was O.W. Gurley, a wealthy black landowner who purchased 40 acres in Tulsa and sold it to other African Americans, fostering a self-sustaining community. The community thrived with schools, hospitals, and newspapers, showcasing the residents' dedication to education and self-reliance.

However, the prosperity of Black Wall Street was tragically cut short. On May 31 and June 1, 1921, the Tulsa Race Massacre occurred, one of the most devastating acts of racial violence in American history. A white mob, enraged by false rumors, attacked Greenwood, burning homes and businesses, and killing an estimated 300 people. The massacre destroyed the thriving district, leaving it in ruins.

Despite the destruction, the spirit of resilience persisted among the survivors. Many residents rebuilt their businesses and homes, and by the mid-20th century, the Greenwood District had regained some of its former prosperity. Today, Black Wall Street stands as a symbol of African American resilience and the ongoing struggle for racial justice.

The legacy of Black Wall Street is commemorated through museums, memorials, and educational programs, ensuring that the history and significance of this remarkable community are not forgotten.

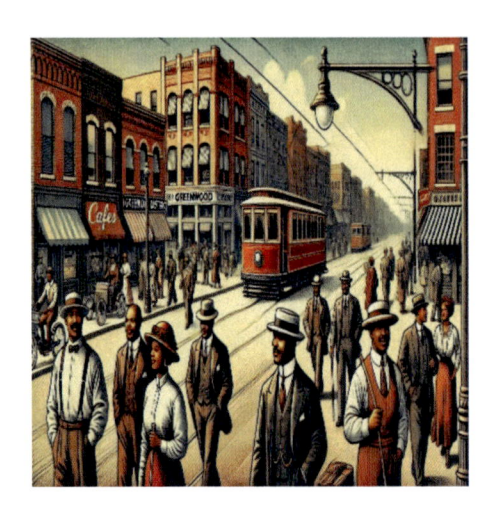

11. Great Plains: Much of Oklahoma lies within the Great Plains region, characterized by flat to rolling terrain.

12. Tallgrass Prairie: The northeastern part of the state is home to the Tallgrass Prairie Preserve, one of the largest protected areas of tallgrass prairie left in the world.

13. Ozark Mountains: The Ozark Mountains extend into northeastern Oklahoma, providing rugged terrain and scenic beauty.

14. Lake Texoma:

Lake Texoma, one of the largest reservoirs in the United States, straddles the border between Oklahoma and Texas. Created by the Denison Dam on the Red River in 1944, it serves multiple purposes, including flood control, water supply, hydroelectric power generation, and recreation.

Covering approximately 89,000 acres, Lake Texoma is a popular destination for outdoor enthusiasts. Its expansive waters and diverse ecosystem support a wide range of activities, such as boating, fishing, swimming, and camping. The lake is renowned for its excellent fishing opportunities, particularly for striped bass, attracting anglers from all over the country.

The surrounding area offers numerous parks, trails, and wildlife refuges. Eisenhower State Park and Lake Texoma State Park provide facilities for picnicking, hiking, and wildlife observation. The Hagerman National Wildlife Refuge, located on the Texas side of the lake, is a haven for bird watchers, featuring a variety of bird species, including migratory waterfowl.

Lake Texoma's creation had a significant impact on the local economy, boosting tourism and providing a reliable water source for nearby communities. The lake also plays a crucial role in regional flood control, mitigating the impact of heavy rains and protecting downstream areas.

The area around Lake Texoma is rich in history and culture. Native American tribes, such as the Chickasaw and Choctaw, have long inhabited the region, and their heritage is reflected in local museums and cultural sites. Additionally, the lake's name combines "Texas" and "Oklahoma," symbolizing the shared heritage and cooperation between the two states.

Lake Texoma continues to be a vital resource and a beloved recreational spot, offering natural beauty and a wide range of activities for visitors of all ages.

15. Red River: The Red River forms the southern boundary between Oklahoma and Texas.

16. Wichita Mountains: This mountain range in southwestern Oklahoma is known for its unique rock formations and diverse wildlife.

17. Black Mesa: The highest point in Oklahoma, Black Mesa, is located in the Panhandle at an elevation of 4,973 feet.

18. Cross Timbers: This ecological region runs through central Oklahoma and is characterized by a mix of prairie and woodland.

19. The 1995 Oklahoma City Bombing:

On April 19, 1995, the heart of Oklahoma City was shattered by one of the deadliest terrorist attacks in American history. At 9:02 a.m., a massive truck bomb exploded outside the Alfred P. Murrah Federal Building, causing widespread devastation and loss of life. The bombing claimed 168 lives, including 19 children, and injured over 600 others. This tragic event profoundly impacted the city and the nation, highlighting the threat of domestic terrorism.

The attack was orchestrated by Timothy McVeigh and Terry Nichols, who harbored anti-government sentiments. McVeigh parked a rental truck filled with explosives outside the federal building and detonated it, causing catastrophic damage to the nine-story structure. The explosion created a 30-foot-wide, 8-foot-deep crater and reduced much of the building to rubble.

The immediate aftermath was chaotic and heart-wrenching. First responders and volunteers worked tirelessly to rescue survivors and recover victims. The incident left a deep scar on the community but also showcased the resilience and solidarity of the people of Oklahoma City. In the days following the bombing, an outpouring of support and aid came from across the nation and around the world.

In the wake of the tragedy, the Oklahoma City National Memorial and Museum was established to honor the victims, survivors, and rescue workers. The Outdoor Symbolic Memorial, located on the former site of the Murrah Building, features 168 empty chairs, each representing a life lost, and a reflecting pool. This site serves as a place of remembrance and reflection, ensuring that the memory of those affected by the bombing lives on.

The Oklahoma City bombing stands as a stark reminder of the dangers of extremism and the importance of community strength and compassion in the face of adversity. It remains a significant event in American history, teaching valuable lessons about resilience, justice, and the power of unity.

20. Arbuckle Mountains: Located in south-central Oklahoma, the Arbuckle Mountains are among the oldest mountain ranges in the United States.

21. Red Earth Festival: This annual festival in Oklahoma City celebrates Native American culture with dance, art, and music.

22. Ouachita Mountains: These mountains extend into southeastern Oklahoma and are known for their dense forests and rugged terrain.

23. Native American Heritage: Oklahoma is home to 39 federally recognized tribes, making it one of the states with the highest Native American populations.

24. Will Rogers: Oklahoma's Favorite Son:

Will Rogers, born on November 4, 1879, in Indian Territory (now Oklahoma), is one of America's most beloved humorists and social commentators. Known for his witty and insightful observations on politics, society, and everyday life, Rogers became a cultural icon in the early 20th century.

Rogers was born into a Cherokee family and grew up on a ranch, where he developed a deep love for horses and the cowboy lifestyle. His early career began in vaudeville, where he showcased his roping skills and comedic talent. His natural charm and humor quickly won over audiences, leading to a successful career in film, radio, and print.

Rogers starred in 71 films, both silent and "talkies," and became a popular radio personality. His syndicated newspaper column, which featured his humorous take on current events, reached millions of readers. Rogers had a unique ability to blend humor with insightful commentary, making him a trusted voice in American households.

Despite his fame, Rogers remained humble and connected to his roots. He often used his platform to advocate for common sense, integrity, and social justice. He famously said, "I never met a man I didn't like," reflecting his belief in the inherent goodness of people.

Tragically, Will Rogers' life was cut short in a plane crash on August 15, 1935, in Alaska, alongside aviator Wiley Post. His death was a profound loss to the nation, but his legacy endures through his timeless wit and wisdom.

The Will Rogers Memorial Museum in Claremore, Oklahoma, preserves his memory and contributions. The museum houses a vast collection of his writings, films, and personal artifacts, offering visitors a glimpse into the life of this remarkable figure. Will Rogers' enduring legacy continues to inspire and entertain, reminding us of the power of humor and kindness in shaping society.

25. Western Swing:
Oklahoma is known for its contributions to Western Swing music, with artists like Bob Wills and His Texas Playboys.

26. The First Yield Sign in Tulsa, Oklahoma:

The first yield sign in the United States was installed in Tulsa, Oklahoma, in 1950. This pioneering traffic control device was the brainchild of Tulsa police officer Clinton Riggs, who recognized the need for a solution to reduce traffic accidents at uncontrolled intersections.

Before the yield sign, intersections were often chaotic and dangerous, with drivers unsure of who had the right of way. Riggs, leveraging his experience in law enforcement and his knowledge of traffic flow, designed the yield sign to address this problem. The original sign was yellow with black lettering and featured the word "Yield" in large letters, along with an inverted triangle, a shape that has become synonymous with the sign to this day.

The first yield sign was placed at the intersection of First Street and Columbia Avenue in Tulsa. Its implementation proved successful, as it significantly reduced the number of accidents at that intersection. The concept quickly gained traction and was adopted by other cities and states, eventually becoming a standard traffic control device nationwide.

The yield sign's introduction marked a significant advancement in traffic safety, providing a clear and straightforward method for managing right-of-way situations. Its success can be attributed to its simplicity and effectiveness in conveying a critical message to drivers, helping to prevent collisions and improve overall traffic flow.

Today, the yield sign is a ubiquitous feature on roads around the world, a credit to the ingenuity of Officer Clinton Riggs and his contribution to public safety. The original yield sign from Tulsa is preserved and displayed at the Tulsa Historical Society and Museum, serving as a reminder of this important milestone in traffic management history.

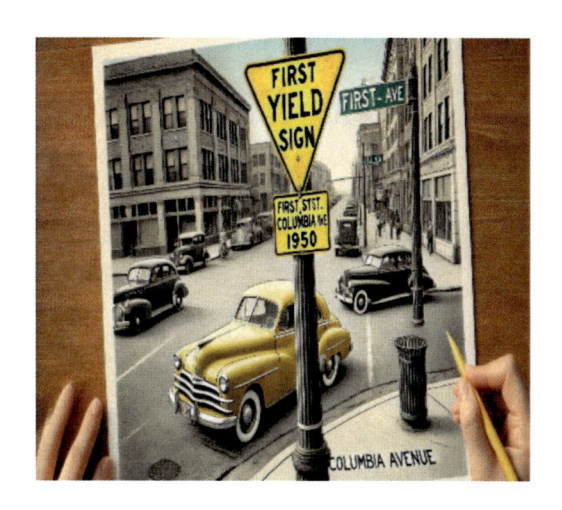

27. Electric Guitar Pioneer: Oklahoma native Charlie Christian is credited with popularizing the electric guitar in jazz music.

28. Woody Guthrie: The legendary folk singer and songwriter was born in Okemah, Oklahoma.

29. First Tornado Warning: The first official tornado warning in the U.S. was issued in Oklahoma in 1948. Oklahoma is known for being in Tornado Alley, with more tornadoes per square mile than any other state.

30. The Invention of the Shopping Cart in Oklahoma City:

The shopping cart, a ubiquitous feature in modern retail stores, was invented in Oklahoma City in 1937 by Sylvan Goldman, owner of the Humpty Dumpty supermarket chain. This innovative creation revolutionized the shopping experience, making it easier for customers to purchase larger quantities of goods and transforming the retail industry.

Before the shopping cart, customers used handheld baskets to carry their items. These baskets quickly became heavy and cumbersome, limiting the amount of merchandise customers could comfortably carry. Goldman, always on the lookout for ways to enhance customer convenience and boost sales, observed this issue and set out to find a solution.

Inspired by a folding chair, Goldman designed a metal frame with wheels and two wire baskets attached. He collaborated with a mechanic, Fred Young, to bring his idea to life. The result was the first shopping cart, which Goldman initially called the "folding basket carrier."

Goldman introduced his invention at his Humpty Dumpty stores, but customers were initially reluctant to use the new contraption. To overcome this, he hired models to push the carts around the store, demonstrating their convenience and ease of use. This clever marketing strategy worked, and soon, customers embraced the shopping cart.

The impact of Goldman's invention was profound. The shopping cart allowed customers to buy more items in a single trip, increasing store sales and transforming the shopping experience. It also led to the development of larger supermarkets and paved the way for modern retail practices.

Sylvan Goldman continued to innovate and improve his design, securing several patents for his shopping cart. His invention remains a cornerstone of the retail industry, highlighting the importance of innovation in meeting consumer needs.

Today, shopping carts come in various designs and materials, but the core concept remains the same. Goldman's invention has stood the test of time, proving to be an indispensable tool in the world of retail.

31. Garth Brooks: One of the best-selling music artists of all time, Garth Brooks is from Tulsa, Oklahoma.

32. Pop Bottle Landmark: The 66-foot-tall soda bottle at Pops in Arcadia, Oklahoma, is a quirky roadside attraction along Route 66. The iconic highway, known as the "Main Street of America," has a significant stretch passing through Oklahoma.

33. Oil Capital of the World: Tulsa was once considered the "Oil Capital of the World" due to its booming oil industry in the early 20th century.

34. The Battle of Honey Springs:

The Battle of Honey Springs, fought on July 17, 1863, was a pivotal conflict in the American Civil War, particularly significant for its location in Indian Territory, now Oklahoma. This battle was notable not only for its strategic importance but also for the diverse composition of its forces.

Union forces, commanded by Major General James G. Blunt, clashed with Confederate troops led by Brigadier General Douglas H. Cooper near Honey Springs Depot. This depot was a vital supply point for the Confederates, making it a key target for the Union. The Union army comprised a unique mix of white soldiers, African American troops from the 1st Kansas Colored Volunteer Infantry, and Native American soldiers from the Creek, Cherokee, and Seminole nations. This diverse coalition reflected the complex allegiances and stakes in the Indian Territory during the Civil War.

The battle began with a fierce exchange of artillery and small arms fire. Despite being outnumbered, the Union forces launched a well-coordinated assault, leveraging their superior artillery and disciplined infantry. The 1st Kansas Colored Volunteer Infantry played a crucial role, demonstrating remarkable bravery and combat effectiveness. Their participation marked one of the earliest significant engagements involving African American troops in the Civil War.

Confederate forces, though initially holding strong defensive positions, eventually succumbed to the relentless Union assault. By the afternoon, they were forced to retreat, abandoning Honey Springs Depot. This Union victory disrupted Confederate supply lines and weakened their control over Indian Territory.

The Battle of Honey Springs is remembered for its strategic impact and as proof of the diverse and unified effort against the Confederacy. The battlefield is now a historic site, preserved to honor the memory of those who fought there and to educate future generations about this critical chapter in American history.

35. Cherokee Nation: The Cherokee Nation, headquartered in Tahlequah, Oklahoma, is the largest of the three federally recognized Cherokee tribes.

36. Green Corn Rebellion: A 1917 uprising by tenant farmers in eastern Oklahoma protesting conscription and economic hardship during World War I.

37. Sequoyah's Syllabary: Sequoyah, a Cherokee from Oklahoma, created the Cherokee syllabary, a writing system for the Cherokee language.

38. State Capitol Dome: The dome of the Oklahoma State Capitol, completed in 2002, features a statue of a Native American warrior named "The Guardian."

39. Oklahoma's Unique Panhandle:

Oklahoma's panhandle is a narrow strip of land extending westward, uniquely distinguishing the state's geography. This 166-mile-long and 34-mile-wide region, often referred to as "No Man's Land," has an intriguing history and plays a significant role in Oklahoma's identity.

The origins of the panhandle date back to the early 19th century. Initially part of Texas, this area became unclaimed when Texas relinquished it in 1850 due to the Missouri Compromise, which prohibited slavery above the 36°30☐ parallel. For several decades, the panhandle was not officially part of any state or territory, earning its moniker "No Man's Land."

During this period, the panhandle became a haven for outlaws, ranchers, and settlers seeking unregulated land. It was a lawless area, with residents forming makeshift governments and community systems to maintain order. In 1890, the Organic Act officially incorporated the panhandle into Oklahoma Territory, bringing it under formal governance and paving the way for its eventual statehood.

The panhandle is characterized by its arid climate and flat, expansive plains. Agriculture, particularly cattle ranching and wheat farming, is the primary economic activity, reflecting the region's rural and rugged nature. The landscape features iconic elements of the American West, such as wide-open spaces, prairies, and mesas.

Culturally, the panhandle has a distinct identity within Oklahoma. It maintains a strong connection to its pioneer roots and the cowboy heritage that defines much of the American West. Small towns in the panhandle, like Guymon and Boise City, embody this unique blend of history and tradition, offering a glimpse into a way of life that remains deeply tied to the land.

Today, Oklahoma's panhandle is celebrated for its unique contribution to the state's geography and history. It stands as a symbol of resilience and adaptability, illustrating how a once-forgotten strip of land became an integral part of the state.

40. Lake Eufaula: The largest lake in Oklahoma, covering 102,000 acres, it is a popular destination for fishing and recreation.

41. Great Salt Plains: Located in northwestern Oklahoma, this area is known for its salt flats and unique selenite crystal digging opportunities.

42. Scenic Byways: Oklahoma has several designated scenic byways, including the Talimena Scenic Drive, known for its breathtaking views of the Ouachita Mountains.

43. The Park-O-Meter: The World's First Parking Meter

The Park-O-Meter, the world's first parking meter, was invented in Oklahoma City, Oklahoma, in 1935. This groundbreaking device revolutionized urban parking management and addressed the growing problem of congested downtown areas due to parked cars. The Park-O-Meter was the brainchild of Carl C. Magee, a lawyer and newspaper publisher who sought a solution to the parking chaos that plagued cities across America.

In the early 1930s, Oklahoma City, like many other cities, faced severe parking issues. Downtown streets were often clogged with parked cars, making it difficult for shoppers and visitors to find available spaces. This congestion hurt local businesses as potential customers struggled to access shops and services. Magee, witnessing these problems firsthand, decided to take action.

Magee's idea was to create a device that would regulate parking by charging a fee for the time a vehicle occupied a space. He collaborated with professors and engineers from Oklahoma State University, and together they developed the Park-O-Meter No. 1. This first parking meter was a simple yet effective mechanism: a coin-operated device that allowed drivers to purchase a set amount of parking time. When the time expired, the meter would display a red flag indicating that the parking time had ended, signaling to traffic enforcement officers that the vehicle was in violation.

The first Park-O-Meter was installed on July 16, 1935, on the corner of First Street and Robinson Avenue in downtown Oklahoma City. The introduction of parking meters was initially met with skepticism and resistance from drivers. However, the benefits quickly became apparent as parking turnover increased, reducing congestion and making it easier for people to find available spaces.

The success of the Park-O-Meter in Oklahoma City led to its adoption in cities across the United States and eventually around the world. The parking meter not only improved urban traffic flow but also generated revenue for city maintenance and infrastructure projects.

Today, parking meters have evolved with technology, incorporating digital payments and smart sensors. However, the core concept remains the same, rooted in Carl Magee's innovative solution from the 1930s. The original Park-O-Meter No. 1 is preserved and displayed at the Oklahoma Historical Society, serving as a very visual and physical example of the city's role in transforming urban parking management.

44. Oklahoma City Thunder: The state's NBA team, originally the Seattle SuperSonics, relocated to Oklahoma City in 2008.

45. Brad Pitt: The Hollywood actor and producer was born in Shawnee, Oklahoma.

46. Astronaut Gordon Cooper: Born in Shawnee, Oklahoma, Cooper was one of the original Mercury astronauts and the first American to sleep in space.

47. The National Cowboy & Western Heritage Museum:

The National Cowboy & Western Heritage Museum, located in Oklahoma City, is one of the premier institutions dedicated to preserving and celebrating the history and culture of the American West. Established in 1955, the museum was initially known as the Cowboy Hall of Fame and Museum. It serves as a vital repository for Western art, artifacts, and cultural history, offering a comprehensive look at the diverse elements that have shaped the West over the centuries.

One of the museum's highlights is its extensive collection of Western art. This includes works by legendary artists such as Frederic Remington and Charles M. Russell, whose paintings and sculptures capture the spirit and rugged beauty of the frontier. Visitors can marvel at the dramatic depictions of cowboys, Native Americans, and expansive landscapes that define the genre.

In addition to its art collections, the museum also houses significant historical artifacts. These include authentic cowboy gear, Native American clothing and tools, and items from famous Western figures like Buffalo Bill Cody and Annie Oakley. The museum's exhibits provide a tangible connection to the past, offering insights into the daily lives and struggles of those who lived in the West.

The museum also features interactive exhibits and educational programs designed to engage visitors of all ages. One such attraction is the Children's Cowboy Corral, where young visitors can learn about the West through hands-on activities and play. There are also live demonstrations, such as traditional cowboy skills like roping and horseback riding, which bring the history and culture of the West to life.

Special events and temporary exhibits ensure that there is always something new to see and experience at the museum. Events like the annual Chuck Wagon Festival celebrate Western heritage with food, music, and crafts, creating a festive atmosphere that draws visitors from all over the country.

The National Cowboy & Western Heritage Museum not only preserves the legacy of the American West but also educates and inspires future generations. Through its rich collections and engaging programs, the museum ensures that the stories and spirit of the West continue to be celebrated and understood.

48. Jim Thorpe: Considered one of the greatest athletes of all time, Jim Thorpe was born in Indian Territory, now part of Oklahoma.

49. Blake Shelton: The country music superstar and television personality was born in Ada, Oklahoma.

50. Geographical Location: Oklahoma is located in the south-central region of the United States, a position that places it at a crossroads of various geographical and cultural influences. It is bordered by six states: Kansas to the north, Missouri to the northeast, Arkansas to the east, Texas to the south and west, New Mexico to the west, and Colorado to the northwest. This unique placement makes Oklahoma a key connector between the Midwest, the Great Plains, and the Southern states.

The state's geography is incredibly diverse, featuring a range of landscapes from prairies and rolling hills to forests and mountain ranges. The eastern part of Oklahoma is characterized by its wooded areas, part of the larger Ozark and Ouachita mountain ranges, which provide a scenic contrast to the flat plains that dominate much of the state's central and western regions. The Great Plains, which stretch across western Oklahoma, are known for their expansive prairies and grasslands, making the area ideal for agriculture and cattle ranching.

Oklahoma is also home to several significant rivers, including the Arkansas River, which flows diagonally across the state from the northwest to the southeast. Other major rivers include the Red River, which forms a natural boundary with Texas, and the Canadian River, which traverses central Oklahoma. These waterways play a crucial role in the state's ecosystem and economy, supporting both agriculture and industry.

The state's climate varies from humid subtropical in the east to semi-arid in the west, contributing to the diverse agricultural outputs from cotton and peanuts to wheat and cattle. Oklahoma's central location also means it is situated in Tornado Alley, a region prone to severe weather, particularly tornadoes during the spring and summer months.

Overall, Oklahoma's geographical location and diverse landscapes make it a unique and integral part of the United States, with its own distinctive blend of natural beauty and cultural heritage.

12

OREGON

1. Nike:

Nike, one of the world's leading sportswear brands, has its roots firmly planted in Oregon. The company was founded in 1964 by Bill Bowerman, a track and field coach at the University of Oregon, and his former student, Phil Knight. Originally named Blue Ribbon Sports, the company started as a distributor for the Japanese shoemaker Onitsuka Tiger (now ASICS). In 1971, they rebranded as Nike, named after the Greek goddess of victory, and introduced the iconic Swoosh logo, designed by graphic design student Carolyn Davidson for just $35.

In the early 1970s, Bill Bowerman revolutionized running shoes by creating a prototype using a waffle iron. Bowerman poured liquid urethane into his wife's waffle iron to create a new sole with a unique waffle-like pattern. This design provided better traction and cushioning for runners. The innovative sole became a defining feature of the Nike Waffle Trainer, a significant breakthrough that helped propel Nike to prominence in the athletic footwear industry.

Nike's headquarters are located in Beaverton, a suburb of Portland, Oregon. The sprawling campus is home to state-of-the-art facilities, including research and development labs, design studios, and sports fields. Nike's influence on sports and culture is immense, pioneering advancements in athletic footwear and apparel. The brand's slogan, "Just Do It," launched in 1988, is one of the most recognizable catchphrases in advertising history.

Nike has signed endorsement deals with some of the biggest names in sports, including Michael Jordan, whose Air Jordan line revolutionized basketball shoes and sneaker culture. Other notable athletes sponsored by Nike include Serena Williams, LeBron James, and Cristiano Ronaldo. These partnerships have helped Nike maintain its position as a leading innovator in athletic performance gear and a cultural icon.

Nike's impact extends beyond sports into social and environmental initiatives. The company has committed to sustainability, aiming to achieve zero carbon and zero waste through initiatives like using recycled materials in products and promoting renewable energy. Nike's efforts to drive change and innovation continue to make it a significant player not only in sports but also in the global effort to create a more sustainable future.

2. Mount Hood: Mount Hood is Oregon's highest peak, standing at 11,240 feet, and is a major destination for skiing and mountaineering.

3. Columbia River Gorge: This scenic area offers stunning waterfalls and hiking trails, including the famous Multnomah Falls, which drops 620 feet.

4. Pacific Coastline: Oregon's coast spans 363 miles, featuring rugged cliffs, sandy beaches, and picturesque lighthouses.

5. Powell's City of Books:

Powell's City of Books, located in Portland, Oregon, is the largest independent bookstore in the world. Established in 1971 by Walter Powell, the bookstore has become an iconic landmark in the city, occupying an entire city block on Burnside Street. With over 1.6 acres of retail space and housing more than one million new and used books, Powell's offers a unique and vast selection that caters to every type of reader.

Walking into Powell's City of Books is like stepping into a literary wonderland. The store is organized into nine color-coded rooms, each dedicated to different genres and subjects, from fiction and non-fiction to rare books and graphic novels. The sheer volume and variety of books available make it a haven for book lovers, and it's easy to spend hours browsing the shelves.

One of Powell's most beloved features is its Rare Book Room, which contains an impressive collection of first editions, signed copies, and other valuable volumes. The store also hosts numerous author events, book signings, and readings, attracting literary enthusiasts from around the world.

In addition to books, Powell's offers a wide range of gifts, stationery, and Portland-themed merchandise. The store's inviting atmosphere and knowledgeable staff create a welcoming environment for both locals and tourists. The coffee shop within Powell's provides a cozy spot for readers to enjoy a cup of coffee while diving into their latest purchase.

Powell's City of Books is more than just a bookstore; it's a cultural institution that reflects the vibrant and eclectic spirit of Portland. It's a place where readers can discover new stories, revisit old favorites, and connect with a community of fellow book lovers. The store's enduring popularity and commitment to fostering a love of reading make it a cherished destination in the Pacific Northwest.

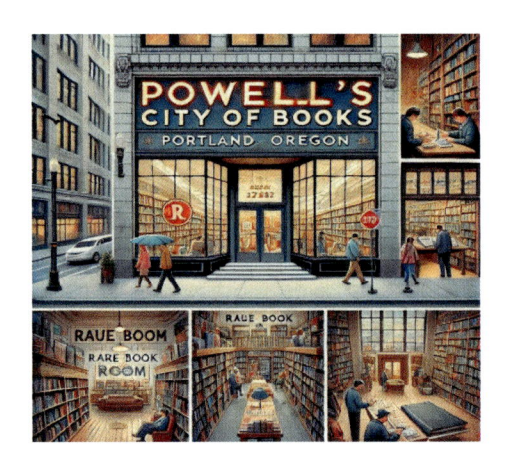

6. Statehood: Oregon became the 33rd state on February 14, 1859.

7. Pendleton Round-Up: This annual rodeo in Pendleton is one of the oldest and most prestigious in the country.

8. Timber Industry: Historically, timber has been a cornerstone of Oregon's economy due to its vast forests.

9. Fishing Industry: Oregon's coast supports a robust fishing industry, particularly for salmon and Dungeness crab.

10. Portland's Bicycle Industry:

Portland, Oregon, is renowned for its vibrant bicycle culture and industry, earning it the nickname "Bike City, USA." The city's commitment to cycling can be traced back to the 1970s when urban planners began to prioritize bike-friendly infrastructure. Today, Portland boasts an extensive network of bike lanes, paths, and boulevards that make it one of the most bike-friendly cities in the United States.

Portland's bicycle industry is a thriving ecosystem of manufacturers, retailers, and advocacy groups. Local bike manufacturers such as Chris King Precision Components and Vanilla Bicycles are known for their high-quality, handcrafted products that attract cyclists from around the world. These companies not only contribute to the local economy but also promote sustainable transportation and innovative bike design.

The city's bike shops, like River City Bicycles and Bike Gallery, offer a wide range of products and services, from basic repairs to custom-built bikes. These shops are community hubs where cyclists gather for group rides, workshops, and events. Portland's robust cycling community is further supported by organizations like the Bicycle Transportation Alliance (now known as The Street Trust), which advocates for safer streets and promotes cycling as a viable transportation option.

Portland hosts several cycling events that draw participants from near and far. The Portland Sunday Parkways, for instance, closes miles of city streets to motorized traffic, allowing cyclists and pedestrians to explore different neighborhoods in a car-free environment. Another notable event is Pedalpalooza, a month-long festival featuring hundreds of themed rides, from the World Naked Bike Ride to food and brewery tours.

The city's commitment to cycling has environmental and social benefits. By promoting bicycles as a primary mode of transportation, Portland reduces traffic congestion, lowers greenhouse gas emissions, and fosters a healthy, active lifestyle among its residents. The bicycle industry in Portland not only supports local businesses but also plays a crucial role in shaping the city's identity and sustainability efforts.

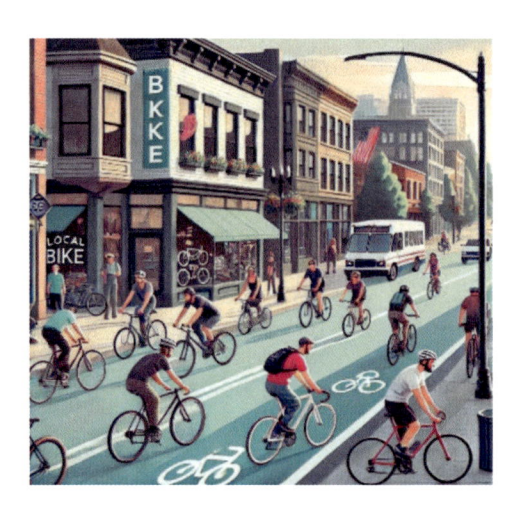

11. Reed College: A liberal arts college in Portland, Reed is known for its rigorous academics and independent study programs.

12. Portland Japanese Garden: One of the most authentic Japanese gardens outside of Japan, located in Portland's Washington Park.

13. Oregon Caves: Located in the Siskiyou Mountains, these marble caves offer guided tours and stunning underground formations.

14. Willamette Valley:

The Willamette Valley, nestled between the Cascade and Coast Mountain Ranges in Oregon, is a lush and fertile region known for its agricultural bounty and scenic beauty. Stretching approximately 150 miles from Portland in the north to Eugene in the south, the valley is home to the state's largest cities and a significant portion of its population.

One of the most renowned aspects of the Willamette Valley is its wine production. The valley's cool climate and diverse soils create ideal conditions for growing a variety of grapes, particularly Pinot Noir. Oregon wines, especially those from the Willamette Valley, have gained international acclaim for their quality and complexity. With over 500 wineries and countless vineyards, the region is a premier destination for wine enthusiasts and connoisseurs.

In addition to its wine industry, the Willamette Valley is a major agricultural hub. The valley produces a wide array of crops, including berries, hazelnuts, hops, and Christmas trees. The fertile soil and moderate climate contribute to the valley's agricultural diversity, making it one of the most productive farming regions in the United States.

The Willamette Valley is also rich in history and culture. The region was a key destination for pioneers traveling the Oregon Trail in the 19th century. Today, visitors can explore historical sites such as the End of the Oregon Trail Interpretive Center in Oregon City. The valley's cities, including Salem (the state capital), Corvallis, and Albany, offer a mix of historical attractions, vibrant arts scenes, and modern amenities.

Outdoor enthusiasts will find plenty to do in the Willamette Valley. The region boasts numerous parks, hiking trails, and rivers ideal for fishing, kayaking, and canoeing. The Willamette River, which flows through the heart of the valley, provides opportunities for water recreation and is a vital part of the local ecosystem.

The Willamette Valley's combination of natural beauty, agricultural richness, and cultural heritage makes it a unique and cherished part of Oregon. Whether exploring its wineries, hiking its trails, or delving into its history, visitors and residents alike are drawn to the valley's diverse offerings and scenic charm.

15. Oregon Zoo: Located in Portland, the Oregon Zoo is the oldest zoo west of the Mississippi River.

16. Wallowa Lake: A glacial lake in northeastern Oregon, surrounded by the Wallowa Mountains, often called the "Alps of Oregon."

17. Matt Groening: The creator of "The Simpsons," Groening was born and raised in Portland.

18. Steve Prefontaine: A legendary middle and long-distance runner, Prefontaine was born in Coos Bay and attended the University of Oregon.

19. Phillips Head Screw:

The Phillips head screw, a cornerstone of modern manufacturing, has intriguing ties to Oregon. Though the invention and initial refinement of the screw were achieved by John P. Thompson and Henry F. Phillips, respectively, its connection to Oregon comes through Phillips, who was a native of Portland.

Henry F. Phillips was born in 1889 in Portland, Oregon. He attended the University of Portland before embarking on a career that would lead to his significant contribution to industry. Phillips' keen business acumen and engineering insights led him to recognize the potential in John P. Thompson's innovative screw design. After purchasing the patent in the early 1930s, Phillips refined and commercialized the screw, ensuring its widespread adoption.

Phillips' improvements to the screw included the introduction of the self-centering cross-head design, which significantly reduced the problem of cam-out, where the screwdriver slips out of the screw head. This innovation was particularly beneficial in the burgeoning automotive industry, where it facilitated more efficient and reliable assembly processes. The first major adoption of the Phillips screw was by General Motors in their Cadillac assembly lines in 1936, which marked the beginning of its rapid integration into manufacturing.

Despite his many achievements, Henry F. Phillips remained connected to his Oregon roots. His pioneering work brought prestige to the state, illustrating how Oregonians have contributed to technological advancements. The Phillips head screw is a prime example of how a seemingly small innovation can have a profound impact on numerous industries worldwide, simplifying construction and manufacturing processes across the globe.

Today, the Phillips head screw is ubiquitous, found in everything from automobiles to electronics to household items. Its enduring success is a testament to Henry F. Phillips' vision and the inventive spirit that characterizes much of Oregon's history. His legacy continues to underscore the importance of practical innovation and its potential to drive significant industrial progress.

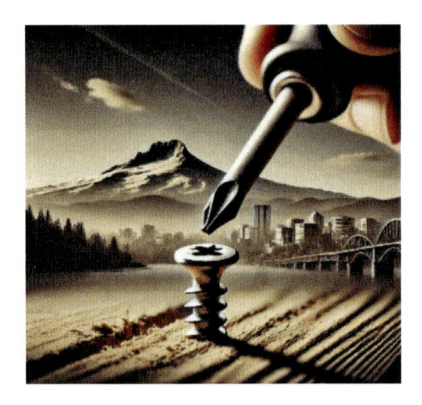

20. Smallest Park in the World: Mill Ends Park in Portland holds the record as the world's smallest park, measuring just 2 feet in diameter.

21. Ken Kesey: The author of "One Flew Over the Cuckoo's Nest," Kesey was an Oregon native and a major figure in the counterculture movement.

22. Voodoo Doughnut: Portland's Voodoo Doughnut is famous for its quirky and unconventional doughnuts, including one topped with bacon and maple.

23. First Drive-Through Espresso Stand: Oregon is credited with opening the first drive-through espresso stand in the United States in Ashland in 1992.

24. International Rose Test Garden:

Nestled in the heart of Portland, Oregon, the International Rose Test Garden is a testament to the city's moniker, "The City of Roses." Established in 1917, the garden is one of the oldest public rose test gardens in the United States. It was created during World War I to preserve European rose species that were threatened by the conflict. Today, it serves as a premier testing ground for new rose varieties, attracting breeders from around the world.

The garden spans over 4.5 acres and is home to more than 10,000 rose bushes representing over 650 varieties. It is divided into several sections, including the Gold Medal Garden, which features award-winning roses, and the Shakespeare Garden, where roses are named after characters from the Bard's plays.

One of the garden's primary functions is to evaluate new rose hybrids for characteristics such as disease resistance, bloom form, color, and fragrance. Roses are sent from breeders globally and are evaluated over a two-year period. Those that perform exceptionally well may receive awards and be introduced to the public.

Visitors to the International Rose Test Garden can enjoy breathtaking views of the roses against the backdrop of the Portland skyline and Mount Hood. The garden is meticulously maintained, offering a serene environment for leisurely strolls and picnics. It is also a popular spot for weddings and photography, providing a picturesque setting with its vibrant blooms and well-manicured landscapes.

The garden hosts the annual Portland Rose Festival, a celebration of the city's rich floral heritage. Events include parades, rose shows, and the crowning of the Rose Festival Queen, further cementing Portland's identity as the City of Roses.

The International Rose Test Garden is not only a beautiful attraction but also a vital part of horticultural science. It continues to contribute to the development of resilient and stunning rose varieties, ensuring that these beloved flowers thrive for generations to come.

25. Tom McCall: The influential governor of Oregon (1967-1975), McCall was known for his environmental policies and the famous "Beach Bill" that ensured public access to Oregon's beaches.

26. Tonya Harding:

Tonya Harding, born on November 12, 1970, in Portland, Oregon, is a former figure skater whose career and life became a dramatic saga of triumph and controversy. Harding rose to prominence in the figure skating world in the late 1980s and early 1990s. Known for her athletic prowess, she was the first American woman to successfully land a triple Axel in competition, a feat she achieved at the 1991 U.S. Figure Skating Championships, where she also won the title.

Harding's career, however, took a notorious turn in 1994, in what became one of the biggest scandals in sports history. Leading up to the U.S. Figure Skating Championships, Harding's main competitor, Nancy Kerrigan, was attacked by a hitman hired by Harding's ex-husband, Jeff Gillooly, and her bodyguard, Shawn Eckardt. Kerrigan was struck on the knee, causing her to withdraw from the competition, which Harding won. The incident led to a media frenzy and a subsequent investigation.

Although Harding denied involvement in the planning of the attack, she eventually pleaded guilty to conspiring to hinder prosecution, admitting she knew about the plot after the fact and did not report it. As a result, she was stripped of her 1994 U.S. Championship title and banned for life from the U.S. Figure Skating Association.

The scandal overshadowed Harding's achievements on the ice, casting a long shadow over her legacy. Despite the controversy, she remains a significant figure in the history of figure skating. Harding's life story, marked by her rise to fame and subsequent fall from grace, was later dramatized in the critically acclaimed film "I, Tonya" (2017), which brought renewed attention to her complex and tumultuous career.

27. James Beard: A celebrated chef and food writer, Beard was born in Portland and is considered the "Dean of American Cookery

28. First State to Decriminalize Marijuana: In 1973, Oregon became the first state to decriminalize the possession of small amounts of marijuana.

29. Hells Canyon: North America's deepest river gorge, Hells Canyon, is deeper than the Grand Canyon and offers breathtaking views.

30. Exploding Whale Incident:

The exploding whale incident is one of Oregon's most bizarre and infamous stories. It took place on November 12, 1970, near the coastal city of Florence. A dead, 45-foot-long sperm whale had washed ashore and started to decompose, causing a significant odor problem. The Oregon Highway Division, tasked with removing the whale, decided to use dynamite to dispose of the carcass.

The plan was to use the explosion to disintegrate the whale into small pieces that would be scavenged by seagulls and other marine animals. Engineer George Thornton was in charge of the operation, and it was determined that half a ton of dynamite would be used. Onlookers, including local residents and a news crew from KATU-TV, gathered to witness the event.

However, the explosion did not go as planned. Instead of vaporizing the whale, the dynamite blasted large chunks of blubber into the air, which rained down on spectators and the surrounding area. A piece of falling debris even crushed a car parked a quarter of a mile away. The majority of the whale remained intact, and the operation ultimately failed to achieve its objective.

The incident quickly became legendary, capturing the public's imagination and becoming a staple of local folklore. The KATU-TV footage of the explosion became a viral sensation decades later when it resurfaced on the internet, cementing the event's place in popular culture.

The exploding whale incident remains a curious chapter in Oregon's history, often cited as an example of what can go wrong with poorly conceived plans. It serves as a reminder of the unpredictable outcomes that can arise from unconventional solutions and continues to be a point of fascination and humor for both Oregonians and the wider public.

31. Oregon Shakespeare Festival: Held annually in Ashland, this festival is one of the oldest and largest professional non-profit theaters in the nation.

32. Salem: The capital of Oregon, Salem, is home to the Oregon State Capitol building, with its unique gold pioneer statue on top.

33. Tech Industry: Oregon's Silicon Forest, particularly around Hillsboro, is home to major tech companies like Intel.

34. Pioneer Courthouse Square:

Pioneer Courthouse Square, often referred to as "Portland's Living Room," is a vibrant public space in the heart of downtown Portland, Oregon. Covering 40,000 square feet, the square is a hub of community activities, cultural events, and a gathering place for residents and visitors alike. Opened in 1984, it is named after the nearby Pioneer Courthouse, a historic federal building dating back to 1869.

The square's creation was a community effort, reflecting Portland's spirit of civic engagement and urban innovation. In the 1970s, a plan to build a parking structure on the site was met with public opposition. Instead, citizens rallied to transform the space into a public square. A design competition was held, and the winning entry by architect Willard Martin featured a design that integrated various elements symbolizing Portland's history and community values.

Pioneer Courthouse Square is paved with bricks, many of which are inscribed with the names of donors who helped fund the project. The square features several iconic elements, including the Weather Machine, a unique sculpture that provides a weather forecast each day at noon, and "Allow Me," a bronze statue of a man with an umbrella. The square's steps and open spaces are designed to accommodate a wide range of events, from concerts and festivals to farmers markets and political rallies.

The square hosts over 300 events annually, making it one of the most active public spaces in the country. It is also home to Portland's official Christmas tree during the holiday season and the popular annual flower festival. The square's design encourages interaction and accessibility, with features like the amphitheater seating and ample space for public art installations.

Pioneer Courthouse Square embodies the essence of Portland: community-oriented, innovative, and welcoming. It is a testament to the city's commitment to public spaces that foster connection and celebrate the local culture.

35. First UFO Sighting: The term "flying saucer" was coined after a UFO sighting by pilot Kenneth Arnold near Mount Rainier in 1947, although he reported it over Oregon.

36. Pioneer of Craft Beer: Widmer Brothers Brewery, founded in Portland in 1984, was among the early pioneers of the craft beer movement in the U.S.

37. Ursula K. Le Guin: The acclaimed science fiction and fantasy author, known for works like "The Left Hand of Darkness," lived in Portland.

38. Crater Lake: Formed over 7,700 years ago, Crater Lake is the deepest lake in the United States, with a depth of 1,949 feet.

39. First City with One-Way Streets: Eugene, Oregon

Eugene, Oregon, holds the distinction of being one of the first cities in the United States to implement a comprehensive system of one-way streets. This urban planning innovation was introduced in the mid-20th century to improve traffic flow and enhance safety in the downtown area.

Before the change, Eugene faced significant traffic congestion, particularly in its central business district. The city planners sought a solution that would streamline vehicle movement and reduce accidents. In 1951, Eugene's city council approved a plan to convert several key streets to one-way traffic. The system was designed to create a more efficient grid, allowing for smoother and faster travel through the city center.

The implementation of one-way streets in Eugene proved to be a success. Traffic congestion decreased, and the rate of accidents dropped significantly. The new system also facilitated better pedestrian movement and encouraged the development of bike lanes, contributing to a more accessible and bike-friendly downtown. The positive impact on traffic management in Eugene set a precedent that other cities across the United States would follow in subsequent years.

Eugene's approach to urban planning has always been progressive, with a focus on sustainability and community well-being. The introduction of one-way streets was part of a broader strategy to create a livable city that prioritizes public safety and efficient transportation. Today, Eugene continues to be known for its innovative urban design and commitment to maintaining a high quality of life for its residents.

The success of the one-way street system in Eugene is a reminder of the importance of thoughtful urban planning. By addressing traffic issues creatively, the city was able to enhance its downtown area, making it more navigable and enjoyable for both residents and visitors. This early innovation in traffic management remains a significant part of Eugene's urban legacy.

40. Oregon Trail: Thousands of pioneers traveled this historic trail in the 19th century to settle in the fertile lands of Oregon.

41. Smith Rock State Park: A premier destination for rock climbing, it's considered the birthplace of modern American sport climbing.

42. John Day Fossil Beds: These fossil beds provide a unique look into prehistoric Oregon with well-preserved plant and animal fossils.

43. The Invention of Plywood:

Plywood, a versatile and essential building material, has its roots in the innovative spirit of Oregon. The invention of modern plywood is credited to Oregon-based industrialist Gustav Carlson, who in 1905 developed a method to create strong, stable panels by layering thin sheets of wood veneer with their grains at right angles. This method, known as cross-graining, significantly increased the strength and stability of the wood, reducing its tendency to split and warp.

Carlson's invention came at a time when the timber industry was booming in the Pacific Northwest. The availability of high-quality timber in Oregon provided the perfect conditions for experimentation and innovation in wood products. Carlson's plywood quickly gained popularity due to its strength, flexibility, and cost-effectiveness. It was first showcased at the 1905 Lewis and Clark Exposition in Portland, where it impressed builders and manufacturers with its potential applications in construction and furniture making.

The use of plywood expanded rapidly in the following decades. During World War II, plywood became a critical material for the construction of military barracks, aircraft, and ships, further proving its durability and versatility. Post-war, the demand for affordable housing and the boom in the construction industry cemented plywood's place as a staple building material.

Today, plywood is ubiquitous, used in a wide range of applications from homebuilding to cabinetry to industrial uses. The invention of plywood not only revolutionized the construction industry but also highlighted the innovative contributions of Oregon's timber sector. Gustav Carlson's pioneering work laid the foundation for the modern use of engineered wood products, showcasing Oregon's pivotal role in the advancement of building materials.

44. Tater Tots: Tater Tots were invented in 1953 by F. Nephi Grigg and Golden Grigg, founders of Ore-Ida. The brothers discovered a way to repurpose potato scraps into crispy, bite-sized cylinders, creating the beloved snack that remains popular today.

45. Tillamook Cheese: The Tillamook County Creamery Association, founded in 1909, is famous for its high-quality dairy products.

46. Agriculture: The state is a top producer of hazelnuts, pears, and blueberries.

47. Marionberries:

Marionberries, often called the "Cabernet of Blackberries," are a unique and delicious fruit that originated in Oregon. Developed by the USDA Agricultural Research Service in cooperation with Oregon State University, the marionberry was released in 1956 and is named after Marion County, where it was extensively tested and cultivated.

The marionberry is a hybrid of two blackberry varieties: the Chehalem and the Olallie. This crossbreeding resulted in a berry that combines the best characteristics of both parents. Marionberries are known for their large size, deep purple color, and complex, rich flavor that balances sweetness and tartness. These berries have a firmer texture and smaller seeds compared to other blackberries, making them particularly appealing for a variety of culinary uses.

Marionberries thrive in Oregon's climate, benefiting from the state's mild temperatures, ample rainfall, and fertile soils. The Willamette Valley, with its ideal growing conditions, is the heart of marionberry production. Oregon produces over 30 million pounds of marionberries each year, making it a significant player in the berry market.

Marionberries are celebrated in Oregon and beyond for their versatility. They are commonly used in jams, jellies, pies, and desserts. Their robust flavor also makes them an excellent choice for sauces, syrups, and even beverages like smoothies and cocktails. The marionberry's prominence in Oregon's culinary scene is highlighted by the annual Marionberry Festival in Salem, where locals and visitors can enjoy a variety of marionberry-based treats.

The development of the marionberry is a clear example of Oregon's agricultural innovation and dedication to producing high-quality, flavorful fruits. This distinctive berry not only contributes to the state's agricultural economy but also embodies the rich agricultural heritage and culinary creativity of Oregon.

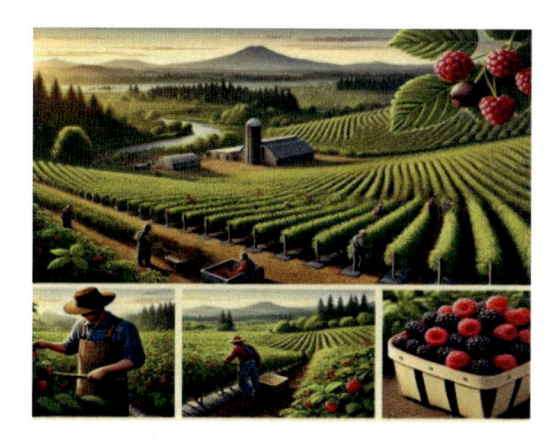

48. Willamette University: Located in Salem, it is the oldest university in the Western United States, founded in 1842.

49. Historic Columbia River Highway: America's first scenic highway, offering stunning views and access to many waterfalls.

50. Geographical Location: Oregon is located in the Pacific Northwest region of the United States. It is bordered by Washington to the north, California to the south, Nevada to the southeast, and Idaho to the east. To the west, Oregon has a coastline along the Pacific Ocean. The state features diverse landscapes, including the Cascade Mountain Range, the fertile Willamette Valley, and extensive forests. Oregon's geographical diversity also includes high desert regions in the east, coastal ranges, and numerous rivers, such as the Columbia and the Snake.

13

PENNSYLVANIA

1. The Declaration of Independence:

The Declaration of Independence, a pivotal document in American history, was adopted on July 4, 1776, by the Continental Congress in Philadelphia, Pennsylvania. This seminal event took place in the Pennsylvania State House, now known as Independence Hall. The Declaration announced the thirteen American colonies' break from British rule and articulated the fundamental principles of freedom and equality.

Drafted primarily by Thomas Jefferson, with input from John Adams, Benjamin Franklin, Roger Sherman, and Robert Livingston, the

Declaration of Independence eloquently expressed the colonies' grievances against King George III. It asserted the inherent rights of individuals, including life, liberty, and the pursuit of happiness. This document was revolutionary, challenging the existing monarchical order and laying the philosophical groundwork for a new nation based on democratic principles.

The adoption of the Declaration of Independence was a bold and risky move for the delegates of the Continental Congress. By signing the document, they were committing treason against the British Crown, risking their lives and properties. Yet, their courage and conviction set the stage for the birth of the United States of America.

Philadelphia, often referred to as the "cradle of liberty," played a crucial role in the nation's founding. Today, Independence Hall and the Liberty Bell remain enduring symbols of American independence and freedom. The Declaration of Independence continues to inspire movements for justice and human rights worldwide, embodying the enduring spirit of the American Revolution.

2. First Capital: Philadelphia served as the first capital of the United States from 1790 to 1800.

3. Liberty Bell: Located in Philadelphia, the Liberty Bell is an iconic symbol of American independence.

4. Delaware Water Gap: This scenic national recreation area along the Delaware River is known for its stunning views and outdoor activities.

5. The Constitutional Convention:

The Constitutional Convention of 1787 was a critical moment in American history, held to address the weaknesses of the Articles of Confederation and to create a stronger federal government. This historic gathering took place from May 25 to September 17, 1787, at the Pennsylvania State House, now known as Independence Hall, in Philadelphia.

Fifty-five delegates from twelve of the thirteen states (Rhode Island did not send representatives) attended the convention. These delegates included some of the most prominent figures of the time, such as George Washington, who presided over the convention, James Madison, Alexander Hamilton, and Benjamin Franklin. Their task was daunting: to draft a new framework of government that would ensure the stability and longevity of the fledgling nation.

The delegates engaged in intense debates and discussions, balancing the need for a strong central government with the protection of individual liberties and state sovereignty. The resulting document, the United States Constitution, established a federal system with a separation of powers among the executive, legislative, and judicial branches. It also provided a system of checks and balances to prevent any one branch from becoming too powerful.

One of the most significant compromises reached during the convention was the Great Compromise, which created a bicameral legislature with representation based on population in the House of Representatives and equal representation for all states in the Senate. Another critical issue addressed was the contentious matter of slavery, leading to the Three-Fifths Compromise, which determined how enslaved individuals would be counted for representation and taxation purposes.

The Constitution was signed on September 17, 1787, and subsequently ratified by the states, becoming the supreme law of the United States. It has since been amended 27 times, with the first ten amendments, known as the Bill of Rights, added in 1791 to guarantee individual liberties.

The Constitutional Convention set the foundation for the United States' system of government, emphasizing democratic principles, the rule of law, and the protection of individual rights. Independence Hall in Philadelphia, where both the Declaration of Independence and the Constitution were debated and signed, remains a powerful symbol of American democracy and governance.

6. Amish Country: Lancaster County is home to a significant Amish community known for their simple living and craftsmanship.

7. Punxsutawney Phil: The famous groundhog from Punxsutawney who predicts the weather every Groundhog Day.

8. Fallingwater: A famous house designed by architect Frank Lloyd Wright, located in the Laurel Highlands of Pennsylvania.

9. Coal Mining: Pennsylvania has a long history of coal mining, particularly in the anthracite coal region of the northeastern part of the state.

10. Gettysburg:

The Battle of Gettysburg, fought from July 1 to July 3, 1863, is one of the most significant events in American history. Located in Gettysburg, Pennsylvania, this battle was a turning point in the American Civil War. The clash between the Union and Confederate forces resulted in the highest number of casualties of the entire war and marked the beginning of the end for the Confederacy.

Gettysburg was strategically important due to its location at the intersection of multiple roads. The Confederate Army, led by General Robert E. Lee, invaded the North, hoping to pressure the Union into peace negotiations or gain foreign recognition. The Union Army, under the command of General George G. Meade, met the Confederates in Gettysburg.

The battle unfolded over three days, with intense fighting at locations such as Little Round Top, Devil's Den, and Pickett's Charge. On the third day, General Lee ordered a massive assault on the Union center at Cemetery Ridge, known as Pickett's Charge. This assault failed disastrously, resulting in severe Confederate losses.

The Union victory at Gettysburg ended Lee's invasion of the North and boosted Northern morale. President Abraham Lincoln later delivered the Gettysburg Address on November 19, 1863, at the dedication of the Soldiers' National Cemetery. In his brief but profound speech, Lincoln emphasized the principles of human equality and the importance of preserving the Union.

Today, Gettysburg is a national park and historic site, attracting millions of visitors annually. The battlefield is preserved with numerous monuments and markers, providing a vivid reminder of the sacrifices made during the Civil War. The Gettysburg National Military Park Museum and Visitor Center offers extensive exhibits and educational programs, ensuring that the legacy of Gettysburg and its pivotal role in American history are remembered and honored.

11. Steel Production: Pittsburgh, known as "Steel City," was once the center of the American steel industry.

12. Will Smith: The famous actor and rapper was born and raised in West Philadelphia.

13. Longwood Gardens: Located in Kennett Square, it spans over 1,077 acres and is one of the most famous botanical gardens in the U.S.

14. Bethlehem Steel:

Bethlehem Steel Corporation, founded in 1904, was once one of the largest and most influential steel producers in the world. Headquartered in Bethlehem, Pennsylvania, the company played a critical role in the industrialization of the United States and the development of modern infrastructure.

Bethlehem Steel's rise to prominence began in the early 20th century under the leadership of Charles M. Schwab, who transformed it into a powerhouse of innovation and production. The company's steel was used in iconic projects such as the Golden Gate Bridge, the Chrysler Building, and the Hoover Dam. Bethlehem Steel also produced the structural framework for New York City's Rockefeller Center and many other skyscrapers, contributing significantly to the urban landscape of America.

During both World Wars, Bethlehem Steel was a vital supplier of steel and munitions to the U.S. military. The company's shipyards produced numerous warships, including battleships and aircraft carriers, which were crucial to the Allied war efforts. This immense contribution earned Bethlehem Steel a reputation as the "Arsenal of Democracy."

The post-war era saw continued success, with the company's steel supporting the booming American automotive and construction industries. However, by the 1970s and 1980s, Bethlehem

Steel faced numerous challenges, including increased global competition, technological changes, and economic shifts. The company struggled to adapt, and in 2001, Bethlehem Steel filed for bankruptcy. Its assets were eventually acquired by the International Steel Group.

Today, the legacy of Bethlehem Steel lives on in the structures it helped build and the communities it shaped. The site of the former Bethlehem Steel plant has been transformed into SteelStacks, a cultural and arts venue that preserves the industrial heritage while fostering new economic and social activities. Bethlehem Steel's story is a testament to the rise and fall of American industry and the enduring impact of innovation and hard work.

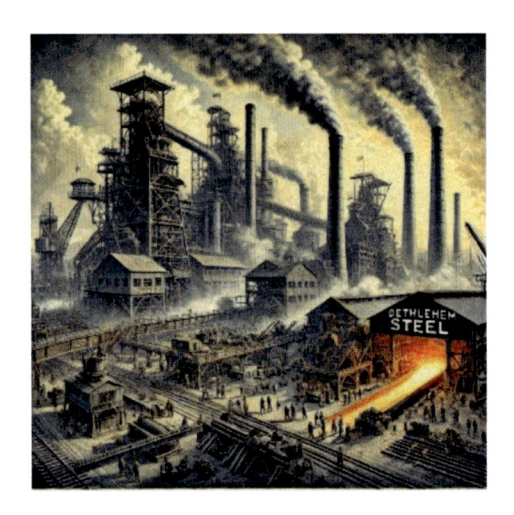

15. Carnegie Library: Pittsburgh's Carnegie Library, opened in 1895, was the first public library funded by Andrew Carnegie.

16. First Bank of the United States: Chartered in 1791 and located in Philadelphia.

17. Natural Gas: The Marcellus Shale formation in Pennsylvania is one of the largest sources of natural gas in the United States.

18. First Zoo: The Philadelphia Zoo, opened in 1874, was the first zoo in the United States.

19. Hershey's Chocolate:

Hershey's Chocolate, founded by Milton S. Hershey in 1894, is one of the most famous chocolate brands in the world. The story of Hershey's Chocolate begins with Milton Hershey's vision to create a utopian town centered around his chocolate factory. He established the town of Hershey, Pennsylvania, where his factory would not only produce chocolate but also provide a thriving community for his workers. This unique approach contributed to Hershey's success and the lasting legacy of the brand.

The Hershey factory itself became a symbol of American innovation and industrial progress. With its iconic smokestacks and production lines, it transformed cocoa beans into delicious chocolate treats enjoyed by millions. Hershey's introduced the first mass-produced milk chocolate bar in America, making chocolate accessible to the general public. The Hershey's brand is now synonymous with quality and delight, producing a wide range of products from chocolate bars to kisses and even theme parks.

Milton Hershey's philanthropic efforts also played a significant role in his legacy. He founded the Milton Hershey School for orphaned boys, providing education and opportunities for those in need. Hershey's commitment to his community and his innovative spirit exemplify the impact one individual can have on both industry and society.

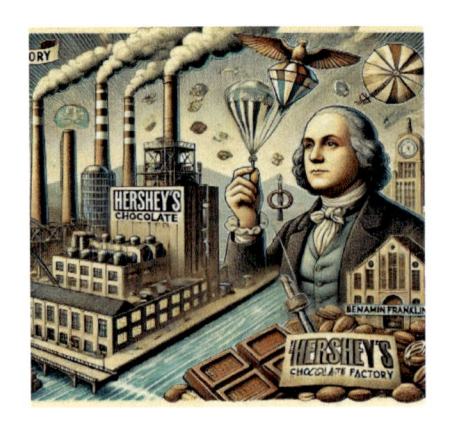

20. Slinky: The iconic toy was invented in 1943 by Richard James in Philadelphia.

21. First Daily Newspaper: America's first daily newspaper, The Pennsylvania Packet and Daily Advertiser, was published in Philadelphia in 1784.

22. First American Flag: Betsy Ross is believed to have sewn the first American flag in her home in Philadelphia in 1776.

23. First Medical School: The University of Pennsylvania founded the first medical school in the United States in 1765.

24. Benjamin Franklin:

Benjamin Franklin was a true Renaissance man of the 18th century, whose contributions spanned science, politics, and literature. Born in 1706 in Boston, Franklin's inquisitive mind and inventive spirit led him to make significant discoveries and advancements. One of his most famous experiments involved flying a kite during a thunderstorm to prove that lightning is a form of electricity. This experiment led to his invention of the lightning rod, a crucial development in protecting buildings from lightning strikes.

Franklin's talents extended beyond science. He was a successful printer, founding the Pennsylvania Gazette and writing the beloved Poor Richard's Almanack, filled with witty aphorisms and practical advice. His contributions to politics were equally profound; he was a key figure in the American Enlightenment, helped draft the Declaration of Independence, and served as a diplomat in France, securing crucial support for the American Revolution.

Franklin also founded several enduring institutions, including the University of Pennsylvania and the first public lending library in America. His inventions, such as bifocals and the Franklin stove, improved daily life for many. Benjamin Franklin's legacy is a testament to his relentless curiosity and dedication to improving society, making him a timeless figure in American history.

25. First Turnpike: The Philadelphia and Lancaster Turnpike, completed in 1795, was the first long-distance paved road in the United States.

26. The First Computer:

The first computer, ENIAC (Electronic Numerical Integrator and Computer), marks the dawn of the digital age. Completed in 1945 at the University of Pennsylvania, ENIAC was a groundbreaking development in computing technology. Unlike modern computers,

ENIAC was enormous, filling a room with its 40 panels and 18,000 vacuum tubes. It was designed to calculate artillery firing tables for the U.S. Army during World War II, significantly speeding up the complex calculations required.

ENIAC could perform 5,000 operations per second, a remarkable feat at the time. It could solve a problem in minutes that would take a human calculator days. This incredible speed opened up new possibilities in science, engineering, and mathematics. ENIAC's development marked a significant shift from mechanical to electronic computing, paving the way for the advanced computers we use today.

The team behind ENIAC included John Mauchly and J. Presper Eckert, who later founded the first computer company. Their work on ENIAC demonstrated the potential of electronic computers, leading to rapid advancements in computing technology and the eventual development of smaller, more powerful machines.

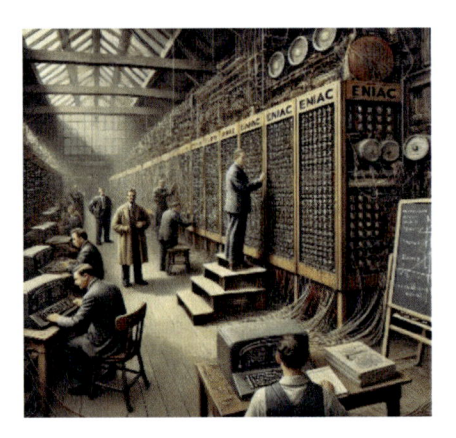

27. KDKA Radio: The world's first commercial radio station, KDKA, began broadcasting in Pittsburgh in 1920.

28. First Art Museum and School: The Pennsylvania Academy of the Fine Arts in Philadelphia, founded in 1805, is the first art museum and school in the U.S.

29. Dr. J: Julius Erving, known as Dr. J, revolutionized basketball with his innovative playing style while playing for the Philadelphia 76ers.

<u>30. Andrew Carnegie:</u>

Andrew Carnegie, born in Scotland in 1835, is a towering figure in American industrial history. Immigrating to the United States with his family as a young boy, Carnegie's rise from a poor immigrant to one of the wealthiest individuals in the world is a classic rags-to-riches story. Carnegie made his fortune in the Pittsburgh steel industry, founding the Carnegie Steel Company, which revolutionized steel production with innovative methods like the Bessemer process. His company played a crucial role in building the infrastructure of America, providing the steel for railroads, bridges, and skyscrapers.

Beyond his industrial achievements, Carnegie was a dedicated philanthropist. He believed in the "Gospel of Wealth," the idea that the rich should use their fortunes to benefit society. This belief led him to donate over $350 million to various causes, a vast sum for his time. His contributions established thousands of public libraries, educational institutions, and foundations, including Carnegie Mellon University and the Carnegie Foundation.

Carnegie's legacy is not just his industrial empire but also his profound impact on education and public resources. His vision that knowledge should be accessible to all led to the creation of over 2,500 libraries worldwide, many of which still bear his name today. His philanthropy set a standard for future generations of wealthy individuals to use their resources for the public good.

31. First U.S. Mint: The first United States Mint was established in Philadelphia in 1792.

32. First World's Fair in the U.S.: The Centennial Exposition of 1876, the first official World's Fair in the United States, was held in Philadelphia.

33. Jimmy Stewart: The Academy Award-winning actor, known for films like "It's a Wonderful Life," was born in Indiana, Pennsylvania.

34. The First Hospital:

The first hospital in the United States, Pennsylvania Hospital, was founded in 1751 by Dr. Thomas Bond and Benjamin Franklin in Philadelphia, Pennsylvania. Inspired by the hospitals in Europe, Franklin and Bond envisioned a facility that would provide medical care to the sick, injured, and mentally ill, regardless of their ability to pay. Their mission was to offer compassionate and effective treatment, reflecting the humanitarian ideals of the Enlightenment.

Pennsylvania Hospital began with a small building that could accommodate a few patients, but it quickly expanded as the need for medical care grew. It was the first institution of its kind in the American colonies, setting the standard for future hospitals. The hospital introduced several innovations in healthcare, including the first medical library in the United States and the establishment of the first surgical amphitheater, where medical students could observe surgeries and learn from experienced physicians.

The hospital's founders emphasized the importance of cleanliness, proper ventilation, and the humane treatment of patients, principles that were revolutionary at the time. Pennsylvania Hospital's legacy continues to influence modern healthcare practices, and it remains a leading medical institution.

35. Arnold Palmer: The legendary golfer, often credited with popularizing the sport, was born in Latrobe, Pennsylvania.

36. First Public Library: The Library Company of Philadelphia, founded by Benjamin Franklin in 1731, is considered the first public library in America.

37. State Parks: Pennsylvania boasts 121 state parks, covering over 300,000 acres.

38. Cherry Springs State Park: Known for its exceptionally dark skies, it's one of the best places for stargazing in the eastern United States.

39. The Philadelphia Stock Exchange:

The Philadelphia Stock Exchange (PHLX) holds a significant place in American financial history as the first organized stock exchange in the United States. Established in 1790, just two years before the

New York Stock Exchange, the PHLX began as a means to facilitate the trading of securities in the burgeoning new nation. Its founding was a testament to Philadelphia's status as a major economic and political center during the early years of the United States.

In the late 18th century, Philadelphia was the largest city in the United States and served as a hub for commerce and finance. The exchange was initially located in the Merchants' Coffee House, where traders and merchants would gather to buy and sell stocks and bonds. This informal setting eventually evolved into a more structured marketplace, with established rules and procedures to ensure fair and orderly trading.

The early days of the Philadelphia Stock Exchange were marked by the trading of government bonds issued to finance the Revolutionary War, as well as shares in various companies, including banks, insurance firms, and transportation enterprises. The exchange played a crucial role in supporting the economic development of the young nation, providing businesses with the capital needed to grow and expand.

Over the centuries, the Philadelphia Stock Exchange has undergone numerous changes, adapting to the evolving financial landscape. It introduced many innovations, such as the first options trading platform in the United States. The exchange continued to grow and modernize, eventually becoming part of the NASDAQ OMX Group in 2008.

Today, the PHLX remains an important player in the financial markets, known for its robust options trading. Its rich history reflects the broader story of American finance, showcasing the growth and transformation of the nation's economic system from its earliest days to the present.

40. Ringing Rocks Park: Located in Bucks County, this park features rocks that emit a bell-like sound when struck.

41. Delaware River: This major river forms the eastern border of Pennsylvania and provides water for over 15 million people.

42. Bushkill Falls: Known as the "Niagara of Pennsylvania," these falls are a series of eight waterfalls in the Pocono Mountains.

43. Andy Warhol:

Andy Warhol, born Andrew Warhola on August 6, 1928, in Pittsburgh, Pennsylvania, was a groundbreaking artist whose influence on modern art is immeasurable. Known as the leading figure in the pop art movement, Warhol's work explored the relationship between artistic expression, culture, and advertisement. His art featured a mix of hand-painted and mass-produced imagery, making bold statements about consumerism and celebrity culture.

Warhol's most iconic works include his silkscreen paintings of Campbell's Soup Cans and portraits of celebrities like Marilyn

Monroe, Elvis Presley, and Elizabeth Taylor. These pieces challenged traditional boundaries between high and low art, blurring the lines between fine art and commercial illustration. Warhol's fascination with mass production led him to adopt mechanical techniques such as screen printing, which allowed him to produce multiple versions of his works.

In the 1960s, Warhol established his famous studio, The Factory, in New York City. The Factory became a hub of creativity and social interaction, attracting a diverse array of artists, musicians, writers, and celebrities. It was known for its eclectic atmosphere, where art, music, and avant-garde performances converged. Warhol's studio was not just a place for creating art but also a cultural phenomenon, embodying the spirit of the 1960s counterculture.

Warhol's impact extended beyond visual art; he was also a filmmaker, author, and record producer. His experimental films, such as "Sleep" and "Empire," pushed the boundaries of conventional cinema, while his collaboration with The Velvet Underground helped shape the music scene of the era.

Despite facing criticism from traditional art circles, Warhol's work has endured, and his influence is still felt today. He redefined the role of the artist in society and opened new avenues for artistic expression. Warhol's legacy lives on through the Andy Warhol Museum in Pittsburgh, the largest museum in the United States dedicated to a single artist, and through the countless artists who continue to draw inspiration from his groundbreaking work.

Andy Warhol's life and work symbolize a transformative period in American art, where the ordinary became extraordinary and the lines between art and life were forever blurred. His unique vision and innovative approach continue to captivate and inspire generations of artists and art lovers around the world.

44. Insurance: Philadelphia is home to many major insurance companies and is a significant hub for the industry.

45. Film Industry: Pennsylvania has been the filming location for many famous movies, including "Rocky," "The Sixth Sense," and "Silver Linings Playbook."

46. Appalachian Mountains: The Appalachian Mountains run through Pennsylvania, offering stunning landscapes and outdoor recreational opportunities.

47. Grace Kelly:

Grace Kelly, born on November 12, 1929, in Philadelphia, Pennsylvania, was a Hollywood icon whose beauty, talent, and grace captured the hearts of millions. She transitioned from a celebrated actress to a beloved princess, leaving an indelible mark on both the entertainment industry and European royalty.

Kelly's acting career began in the early 1950s, and she quickly rose to fame with her performances in films like "High Noon" (1952), "Dial M for Murder" (1954), and "Rear Window" (1954). Her collaboration with director Alfred Hitchcock solidified her status as a leading lady in Hollywood. Known for her poise and elegance, Kelly won the Academy Award for Best Actress for her role in "The Country Girl" (1954), showcasing her versatility and depth as an actress.

Her life took a fairy-tale turn when she met Prince Rainier III of Monaco at the Cannes Film Festival in 1955. The couple married in a lavish ceremony on April 19, 1956, and Kelly became Princess Grace of Monaco. Her transition from Hollywood starlet to European royalty captivated the world and brought significant attention to the small principality of Monaco.

As princess, Grace Kelly dedicated herself to charitable work and the arts. She founded the Princess Grace Foundation to support local artisans and promote cultural projects. Her commitment to philanthropy and her role in elevating Monaco's cultural scene earned her immense respect and admiration.

Grace Kelly's legacy extends beyond her filmography and royal duties. She embodied timeless elegance and grace, influencing fashion and style for decades. Her impact is still felt today, with numerous tributes in film, fashion, and popular culture.

Tragically, Kelly's life was cut short in 1982 when she suffered a stroke while driving and passed away following a car accident. Her death was a significant loss, but her legacy endures through her contributions to film, her philanthropic efforts, and the enduring allure of her life story.

Grace Kelly's transformation from Hollywood star to royal icon remains one of the most enchanting narratives of the 20th century. Her story continues to inspire and fascinate, celebrating a life marked by elegance, talent, and a commitment to making a difference.

48. Susquehanna River: The longest river on the East Coast of the United States that flows into the Atlantic Ocean, it is a vital waterway in Pennsylvania.

49. Ohiopyle State Park: Known for its waterfalls, rapids, and white-water rafting on the Youghiogheny River.

50. Geographical Location: Pennsylvania, often referred to as the Keystone State, is located in the northeastern region of the United States. It is one of the original 13 colonies and has a rich history and diverse geography.

Bordering Pennsylvania are six states: New York to the north, New Jersey to the east, Delaware to the southeast, Maryland to the south, West Virginia to the southwest, and Ohio to the west. Additionally, Pennsylvania has a 57-mile shoreline along Lake Erie to the northwest, providing access to one of the Great Lakes.

The state covers a varied landscape, stretching approximately 283 miles from east to west and about 160 miles from north to south. Eastern Pennsylvania is dominated by the Delaware River, which forms the border with New Jersey. The Appalachian Mountains run diagonally through the state, adding to its diverse topography with ridges and valleys. To the west, the landscape transitions into the rolling hills and valleys of the Allegheny Plateau.

Philadelphia, Pennsylvania's largest city, is located in the southeastern part of the state, near the confluence of the Delaware and Schuylkill rivers. Pittsburgh, another major city, lies in the southwestern part, at the meeting point of the Allegheny, Monongahela, and Ohio rivers.

The state's central region is known for its agricultural productivity and contains the fertile Susquehanna Valley, through which the Susquehanna River flows from the northeast to the Chesapeake Bay in Maryland. Pennsylvania's diverse geography contributes to its climate, which varies from humid continental in most of the state to humid subtropical in the southeast.

Pennsylvania's location and geographical features have played significant roles in its economic development, historical significance, and cultural heritage, making it a pivotal state in the American landscape.